PRAYED OUT

John Michael Hanvey

Prayed Out

GOD IN DARK PLACES

the columba press

First published in 2005 by
the columba press
55A Spruce Avenue, Stillorgan Industrial Park,
Blackrock, Co Dublin

Cover by Anú Design
Origination by The Columba Press
Printed in Ireland by ColourBooks Ltd, Dublin

ISBN 1 85607 505 2

Acknowledgements
The author and publisher are grateful to the following for permission to quote from copyright material: J. M. Dent, a division of the Orion Publishing Group, for quotations from *Collected Poems by R. S. Thomas*; 'Sadness' from *Between Angels* by Stephen Dunn. Copyright © 1989 by Stephen Dunn. Used by permission of W. W. Norton & Company Inc; 'Happiness' by Raymond Carver from *All of Us: Collected Poems*, published by Harvill Press. Used by permission of The Random House group Ltd; Penguin Books for a quotation from Elie Wiesel's *Night*.

Table of Contents

Preface

In 1966 I was 18. That year I was clothed with the habit of the Franciscan Order and was symbolically told, as the Provincial put the habit on me, that I was dying to the old Adam and putting on the new. It all made so much sense, after a rather turbulent adolescence.

I had been inspired by the life of St Francis and I was attracted to the idea of working for the poor. It was a similar inspiration that drew me on to ordination, 'To bring good news to the poor.'

The poor were very real to me. My family was amongst the post-war poor of a Lancashire mill town and all the people who went to our church and school struggled with poverty.

Thanks to the example and inspiration of a certain Jesuit priest in our parish, I never saw priesthood in any way related to power or status but rather being at the tough end of service and prayer. I was one of the fortunate young people to have someone saintly and scholarly as my priest.

Now, thirty-seven years on from those youthful and confident steps into religious life and priesthood, I find myself in unexpected territory. What was once my base for living has now become almost unrecognisable. The familiar landmarks don't always make that much sense anymore and I find myself, when I'm really honest, in a place of desolation with not even a lock of God's hair to prove that I've been on a life-long journey searching for him. I find myself at the crossroads waiting for God to speak to me again, like he used to when I was young. His long silences and my less and less understanding of him sometimes worry me.

When all this began to happen, it felt like abandonment. Strangely, I could cope with the possible abandonment of other human beings, but by him to whom I had given everything since I was eighteen, I found difficult to handle; and I couldn't find too many 'Masters in Israel' to interpret this to me. Up till this moment, I was driven by what I thought was God. I did all the right things: I prayed, prepared well my preaching and liturgy, and set out each day to be a compassionate man who followed St Ignatius' advice: 'To give and not to count the cost, to fight and not to heed the wounds.'

God was intervening in my life in a way I did not want him to and I felt he was getting in the way of *my* ministry. It's embarrassing now to think that I actually believed that it was *mine*. I had often preached that God had the habit of breaking into people's lives in disturbing ways and taking away familiar and comfortable things in order that they did not lose that which was really important. But why he should be doing this to me at this time was incomprehensible.

And so I took him on with the arrogance of youth and wrestled with him like Jacob did in the night. I was left nursing my pain and desolation, with a real absence and deep-down sense of failure – failure as a man and as a priest.

For a long time the feelings that accompanied this were negative and angry. I felt cheated by God. All that had gone before seemed to count for nothing. I turned my anger inward and was quite self-destructive. No matter how much help I was offered, no matter how much love, nothing of any positive significance seemed to happen. Whatever it was, it seemed intractable. Where once I found all my strength, my hope, my meaning, I now felt darkness and deep down sorrow. As the boom of Job says: 'How long will you torment me and crush me ...? My harp is tguned to mourning and my flute to the sound of wailing.' (Job 19:1, 30, 31)

At this stage, spiritual things – prayer, liturgy – were luxuries I couldn't afford. I felt I was fighting for my very life. The images of God I'd had for years now felt obsolete; no comfort in this faith anymore. What happened in this 'prayed out' period of my life is what this book is about. The shame and the pain of things that I never thought possible, actually happened.

I hung on with one hand to what had been, with bleeding fingernails and with the other I stretched out to try and touch heaven by the hem, hoping against hope. Then the events of my life brought me into some uncharted territory. By this time, I had given up trying anymore to work out things and with God, I was barely on speaking terms. I began to shut down emotionally.

From here I found myself, by what I now choose to call the irony of God's workings, amongst those at the very edges of society. The Project I now belong to is called T.H.O.M.A.S. (Those on the Margins of a Society): the homeless, young people addicted to drugs, the abused and neglected, people whose minds have been fractured by life – who feel it isn't worth living – and act accordingly. Whilst I acknowledge that those of us who form the community at T.H.O.M.A.S. are not living in any Utopia, it was here I felt I heard the gospel as if for the first time. Not preached to me by bishops and priests but by the poor themselves.

I began to realise that God had taken me to a different priestly ministry but one which I had subconsciously wanted ever since I was eighteen. It was an expression of priesthood that was about standing alongside people as a brother and friend. It drew me back to a deeper personal prayer life where intercession, that great priestly calling, was more and more present to me. I found myself fulfilling that part of me that is Franciscan, more and more, almost at times in spite of myself. But it was no Damascus road experience for me. I still struggle with my fragile humanity and my sometimes poor response to my different priestly ministry. But I do feel here a more profound, albeit broken love, than I've experienced in more traditional religious community. God seemed to be saying to me: 'Don't go back, risk. Let the props go that kept you outwardly strong. Lean on me. Let me take you to an alien land and know that when you are weak you are strong.'

I am now no longer working for the poor and those on the edges of life, I am poor and on the edge myself. This is the gift that God has given me. I stress that it has been given, because I would never have volunteered for this. Incarnation is taking place, with its indistinguishable mixture of both birth and death. I am much more comfortable with my flesh-bound spirituality.

My poverty is much more up front with God and with others. I
don't much ask the question 'why?' these days, rather I wait before my often-absent God. For me, it seems that the meaning is
in the waiting and the poor always have to wait.

This book is about my journey. I write it without resentment
and have no intention to scandalise people who read it. But this
is my real story and in it there is the truth that both challenges
and disturbs.

I write it also because I know priests and other people who
struggle in deep loneliness and sometimes despair. My wish is
that this book will be one of hope, liberation and unbinding. I
want it to be a spiritual and theological meditation on the extravagant love of God for each of us no matter where our journey has taken us.

As I write this, the church is going through its own terrible
struggle with its demons, where cardinals and bishops are re-
signing and priests being sent to prison. My story, like the
church's, is no easy ride – and no easy read. It is, rather, in the
Jungian tradition of facing head-on the darkness and it seems to
be the only way forward. When Jesus headed for Jerusalem,
where the desolations and derelictions of the cross were waiting,
we are told that he set out resolutely for that place and 'set his
face like flint'.

The book begins with a parable and the chapters which follow develop the themes of the parable and no matter what,
whether 'prayed out' or 'unfaithful', always offering the extravagant gift of redemption. As St Bernard of Clairvaux writes, 'He
came to pay a debt he did not owe, for us who had a debt we
could not pay'.

CHAPTER ONE

Redemption – Mass for the Dead – A Parable

He has made me dwell in darkness like those long dead ...
yet I have hope. (Lamentations 3:6, 21)

It doesn't take long to get drunk. He had two hours to kill before the coach taking him north left Victoria. He paced up and down outside a nearby pub in a well-practised, empty and painful ritual. There was a small voice telling him not to go in, intellectually he knew he shouldn't. But the other voice, much stronger and eminently more attractive, especially on a winter's afternoon, beckoned him inside. He'd managed to get through the whole of Christmas without a drink. New Year had gone by finding him stone cold sober. But he knew what he was going to do. He was loitering with intent and that London pub spoke to him of comfort and good times. He noticed little of the downmarket décor as he made his way to the bar, almost like a man driven, having to do what he had to do quickly. He ordered a large Southern Comfort which he swallowed Russian style and then asked for another. The battle was over. The first drink had hit him. What followed was inevitable. He drank the second and ordered again.

As he came from the bar to sit down, he glanced through the window and noticed that it had started to snow. He hoped in a sort of childlike way that it would fall hard enough for him to phone north to explain why he would be arriving late. Or better still why he couldn't be there at all. He opened the telegram and re-read the now familiar words:

Tried to phone ... No luck ... Mother died today ... Funeral Friday 10 am ... Reception of body to church Thursday 7 pm ... presume you will conduct both Reception and Requiem ... Mike

He'd finished the third double and was mildly embarrassed enough to leave that pub and make his way to another one, in case the barman thought he might be drinking too much too quickly.

It was snowing quite hard and he knew he would need something to keep out the cold for the unbearably long, dry coach journey. He saw a deli. He smiled at the young Asian who served him the bottle of scotch. 'Having some friends round?' he asked. As if he needed to offer a reason for his purchase. As if anyone cared.

He went quickly into the next bar and ordered a large Southern Comfort. After a sip, he went to the gents with his overnight bag containing the bottle of scotch. He could always buy another for the journey. He was just about to open the bottle when someone entered the cubicle next door to him. This irritated him. In order to break the seal on the bottle he had to both cough and pull the chain so the guy next door wouldn't hear the tell-tale crack. He sat down and drank. The best part of a quarter met the rest and flowed around inside his veins making him feel alive, almost normal, as he understood it. Ready for anything. Hoping to meet and connect. He read some of the graffiti on the wall and wondered if people ever did meet in such places. He went back to his large drink and could now sip like ordinary drinkers, who popped in for a quick one on their way home from work.

By now the alcohol had released some ghosts that came into his mind, uninvited. He could even feel a little emotion now for the woman he called 'Mother', who was dead, and tried to en-gage in conversation with a disinterested drinker with half a bit-ter in front of him, telling him the purpose of his journey north. Another trip to the loo; another good belt from the bottle and an-other large one from the bar.

He remembered ordering that drink but the rest was vague. When he did 'come to', to say 'wake' would make it sound too pleasant, he found himself sitting on a bench, in the small park across from the Grosvener Hotel. He staggered to his feet like a snowman coming to life, in a frightening fairy story. His overnight bag was missing, stolen, lost. He looked at his watch and of course, had missed his coach north. He was used to missing things. He felt panic. A deep fear in his gut, mixed with self-loathing and anger. It was already well past 7 pm and her body would now be in the church with all the family present, except him. He weaved his way up to the coach station to negotiate a ticket for the night coach. He thought he'd better not phone home in case they detected that he was far from sober. He knew that they would already have deduced that anyway. He looked at his watch and noticed that he had about three hours to wait till the night coach. There was no chance of him living with himself for that long. He had to kill the pain and he knew only one way.

He opened his eyes and found himself sitting on a National Express that was making its way through the snowy night. He didn't remember boarding at Victoria, and wondered were he might be heading. He'd been in this space before and had learned it was part of the way his life just was. He had no more alcohol. He felt the usual feelings of shame, low self-worth and panic, and he craved only one thing. He noticed through the snowstorm a sign saying 'North'. So he was heading home at last, almost by accident. He had not been back for years. Now the dead hand of a woman he had called 'Mother' was beckoning him back. She wasn't his natural mother. As he thought of her, his mind went back further, and the phantoms of the night that only the addict knows, turned on him and forced him to where he would rather not go. It had been a northern youth, with mill sounds and clogs and a hissing gas light in the bedroom. It had been hot-water bottles and ice-cold sheets and the empty never-used fireplace in his room. It was the smell of the coalman's horses' breath. It was Mr Price the undertaker who later committed suicide. It was a Catholic youth, with incense smells and candles. And darkness. And a red lamp burning into him, that God was present. It was Catholic teachers, who all looked the same – old, thin and very holy, who told him to join his hands and close his eyes. It was a district nurse youth, who checked his hair and put wooden spatulas onto his tongue. It was school photographs and chapped legs and short trousers that were never really short. It was a bookless youth, with only dreams to play with. But most of all it was 'her'. There was a bond, an almost unspoken secret relationship between him and his mother. She became ill suddenly, so it seemed to him. Though she had done some strange things, like wandering off at night in her bedroom slippers with her shopping basket. She had sometimes gone to the pub and ordered tea. They knew her and brought her home. One summer holiday after he had come in from playing and gone into the kitchen, he found her standing on a chair, with a rope fixed to a hook in the ceiling. He held her legs tight to his face and wet them with his tears.

It was when she became incontinent that his father had to put her in a home. It wasn't long before she was dead. They told him she had fallen, but when he kissed her in her coffin, she had white bandages all around her neck up to her chin. He remembered the summer, and the rope, and the tears.

His father spent the remainder of his short life chasing drunkenness, till he died from alcoholic poisoning. He had found him by the side of his bed. He was taken away in a metal coffin. From out of the blue, a new mother came, a distant aunt. She took him and his younger brother Mike to her own home. His phantoms, like the ghost of Christmas past, forced him to gaze back on his dead, unloved father. He remembered how big his hands looked in the coffin, and it was raining outside. When he walked out into the wet streets of that old mill town, he had thought that maybe his God was away just a while, and he would be back soon.

By the time the coach pulled into the bus station he was sober, at least by his standards. He'd had to change the goal posts many times. Now sober meant he could stand up and not fall over. It was 7.30 am and still snowing, and he needed a drink. He'd never get through the Requiem Mass without one. Nothing opened before 8.30. It meant he would have to take a later bus to his home town, 12 miles away. Only just getting him to the church by 10 o'clock, plus the problem of the snow. He walked up and down some side streets hoping that maybe at least one shop was open, and at last he found one. It sold everything. The boy behind the counter was not unlike the Asian who had served him in London. He nervously asked for a bottle of scotch. The boy, without a change of facial expression, put it into a brown paper bag. Outside, he couldn't be bothered finding a toilet to drink in. He opened the bottle in the street and drank straight from the neck. Within minutes, his shaking began to stop and his body began to feel normal again and the phantoms of the night had been exorcised.

The candles were already burning, both on the altar and by the coffin. The wine was already in the cruet and the congregation seated. When he arrived, his younger brother Mike was trudging around in the snow. When Mike saw him, he swore at him and told him he could smell whisky on his breath. After a few words of assurance, he left Mike and went to the sacristy to vest for Mass. Mike told the rest of the family that 'Angel' had arrived and hoped he would not embarrass the family. 'Angel' was the name given him by the only other person he had loved, beside his mother – Lorenzo who had given meaning to his broken life.

'Angel' stood in the sacristy, where he had served Mass as a boy. In fact every step of his spiritual journey had been celebrated in that church, Baptism, First Confession, First Communion, Confirmation and Ordination to the Priesthood. He stood at the vestment press and knew that it was to be for the last time. It had been 20 years since he had last stood there and then he had been young and sober and not as lustful as he had become. He had not experienced love then either, or loved anyone in return, except that short and broken love between him and his mother. It was five minutes to ten, the three altar boys were almost ready and were chattering about when to light the charcoal for the incense and who was going to stand at the head of the coffin with the cross. As he vested, he knew that he would never again bend over the bread and wine and consecrate them into Christ's body and blood. This was his last Mass. He was glad that it was a Mass for the Dead and that it was in the church of his youth where his 'real' mother had brought him at six days old and where over the years, had taught him the profound nature of the Sacrifice, which even as a youth, he marvelled at. Like many young people he had lost his faith in his teens but, not being able to fill the chasm with sex or anything else on the 60s menu, he returned to be one of its ambassadors and he was good. He had all the gifts and he could communicate with both the young and the old. The young saw him as young in his thinking and were surprised at his black humour; the old could talk to him about their aging problems and their aches, pains and doubts, as they approached the end of their lives; they knew he understood. The only person who didn't like him was himself; this was part of his curse and now at this moment he never hated himself more. Already he knew what he was going to do.

He bowed to the crucified God as if giving a knowing nod to an old colleague, then turned to the altar boys and said, as he had often said before to such boys to help them feel at ease and get a smile, 'Let's get this show on the road.' The congregation stood as the sacristy bell rang and out came the small procession. 'Angel' joined his hands in a posture of prayer and noticed how dirty his nails were, and that his hands had started to tremble again. He kissed the stone altar as a mark of reverence for the place of sacrifice and started the sacred rite. His voice was strong and confident and he spoke with power – even without the whisky he spoke well, but with it, as long as he was just not over the limit for preaching, it was a voice that touched the hearts of his hearers. 'Angel' sat down to wait for the altar to be prepared for the offertory and to wait for the gifts of bread and wine to be brought up in procession. He caught a young Italian boy's face. He was the adopted son of a member of the family. His dark, vibrant features brought back memories of another face which he pushed painfully away. He desperately needed a drink. He was only half way through and he needed alcohol. The sweat began to pour down his face and made his glasses slip down his nose. His whole body was soaked and the shaking was worse. He was far enough away for the congregation not to notice these details but he felt that they were staring at him. The offertory hymn was still being sung so he had time to 'do the deed'. He pulled out his handkerchief, started coughing uncontrollably, then he quickly left the sanctuary through the side door and went straight to the cupboard where the altar wine was kept. He pulled the cork out of the sherry bottle and drank over a quarter of it. His eyes watered, he breathed heavily. Then another swig and he quickly returned to his chair, feeling guilt, shame and revulsion and at the same time relief. He just hoped that by the time the funeral was over he was not staggering or slurring his words. Speed was essential, for he could no longer be sure of endings. He rattled on until, as always for him, he came to that moment when even with his battered and god-forsaken faith, he knew that what he was about to do would make God present.

This drunken, unfaithful, lustful, broken man was about to summon the Lord of All into his shaking and nicotine stained hands. He pronounced the words slowly as if for the first time. He held the bread and breathed alcohol onto it saying 'This is my Body given for you'. He raised the host high as if reaching to the heavens in desperation, begging almost just to touch the hem of God, just waiting for a movement from behind the curtain indicating that someone might be there. He then took the chalice. To his utter disgust and shame, he looked at that which was to become the Blood of Christ and saw only alcohol to drink. 'This is the cup of my Blood, the Blood of the new and everlasting covenant. It will be shed for you and for all so that sins may be forgiven. Do this in memory of me.' His hands were still shaking as he gave out communion. Then he quickly drew the Mass to its conclusion and began the obsequies at the coffin. He blessed and incensed the coffin, almost disappearing in the billowing smoke. He had fulfilled his promise to the woman he called mother from the age of 14 and hadn't seen for 20 years. As he led the coffin up the aisle to the waiting hearse, he thought of those 20 years – when alcohol was not a problem for him.

He also remembered the one, the only one, apart from his mother who loved him. He had even more unwelcome time to think and remember as the funeral car, which he and the altar boys occupied, drove them to the cemetery. The young Italian smiled at one of the boys as he made faces through the window of the limousine as it left the churchyard. He reminded him of Lorenzo – who had renamed him 'Angel' after the doomed Angel Clair in the Thomas Hardy novel *Tess of the D'Ubervilles*.

It had been two years ago since this boy breathed into his declining life. It had been a Friday lunchtime in the East End of London. He went to the door and saw a picture of beauty and pain. Lorenzo told him of how he was in a squat, of how he was hungry and needed money, of how his girlfriend had gone, and how once he used to use drugs. They talked about Italy and they ate. Lorenzo ate quickly and drank Coca-Cola. When he had finished, 'Angel' gave him £10 and shook hands. Before Lorenzo reached the door he vomited and began to sweat. The local surgery was closed so 'Angel' took him to the outpatients' department of the local hospital. After 5 hours of tests and examinations, 'Angel' was called in and Lorenzo told him he was HIV positive. 'Angel', because he was compassionate and more than aware of his own intrinsic brokenness and weakness, saw the half-naked emaciated body as a sort of piéta and held him in reassurance and love. After some time in the Middlesex hospital, 'Angel' invited Lorenzo to live in the presbytery. The bishop, when he found out, disapproved and told him to make alternative arrangements. For Angel, the very reason for getting up in the morning was Lorenzo; even his drinking had decreased since he had been there. This was a pure love. Not the lustful empty experiences that were familiar to 'Angel'. 'Angel' was a little embarrassed at the outward affection of Lorenzo who would not think twice about a hug or arms around the shoulders in public. This was unfamiliar territory for 'Angel' and it was love that had come too late. Already the existential loneliness had led 'Angel' into other ways of taking away the pain and he knew that even if he were capable of loving Lorenzo in return,

Lorenzo deserved someone better. 'Angel' knew he was almost a hopeless case, he knew also that existential loneliness was always to be his lot; it had been with him since the age of reason. If Lorenzo should get full blown AIDS, even if he wanted to help him, he would not be able to do so. He was too far gone on the despairing road. Difficult though it was, 'Angel' tried to let Lorenzo go, even encouraged him to go, maybe he could find a girl to love him again, but both 'Angel' and Lorenzo knew that in his present condition it was unlikely.

Lorenzo was for living *now*, the present moment. There was no lust here for 'Angel', he'd known the loneliness of that. This must be love. After some time Lorenzo talked about 'Angel' packing everything in and going with him to Italy. Even though his priesthood was in ruins, he was too frightened to leave and start again, even though he wanted to. He had made all sorts of strange sacrifices throughout his life for others, in order that they might reach the kingdom of heaven and maybe help him to do the same. But he had grown accustomed to living among the ruins of his vocation. He knew that he would hurt Lorenzo if he went with him, but also knew that he would destroy himself, with or without him.

The day that Lorenzo left for Italy, 'Angel' went with him to the airport; he had never felt such inner pain before. It was the emptiness and loneliness of death. They hugged and kissed and 'Angel' gave Lorenzo an envelope with five thousand pounds in it, most of his savings.

As 'Angel' made his way to one of the airport bars, he felt that his 34 years had been worthwhile just for Lorenzo, but he could cope even less now that he was not there. There was no physical presence, and memory was not enough. 'Angel' needed him to be there all the time. An assurance that there was still some worth in him and that he was not alone. They never met again.

When 'Angel' moved out of the parish at the bishop's request because of his increased drinking, he moved into a rather dingy bed-sit and he told no-one, except his brother Mike, where he was so any letters Lorenzo might have sent were never forwarded.

They reached the cemetery and it looked quite beautiful in the shroud of snow. Luckily for 'Angel' he could still walk straight and he practised speaking to himself and found he was not slurring his words. Everything was white, and then he saw the gaping hole of the grave, black against the freshly fallen snow. He had seen open graves many times before but today this deep pit beckoned him, as if calling him home. At last everything was over. Mass for the Dead had been offered and the committal was finished. There was a reception at one of the good hotels in the town but 'Angel' decided not to go there. They drank far too slowly on these occasions anyway.

He returned to the church and took off his vestments and slowly put on his overcoat. He gave some money to the three altar boys and thanked them. One of the boys told him that he was going to become a priest one day. 'Angel' looked at him and said nothing.

Angel went straight from the church to the off-licence and bought a bottle of scotch. He then made his way to the chemist and purchased a bottle of paracetemol. Then it was back to the now empty church. He entered the priest's side of the confessional. Here would be the place where mercy could be found, even for him. He looked at the purple silk stole of the priest, discoloured with age, thrown quite casually over the back of the chair and thought back to his first confession made just inches away on the other side of the confessional grill. And now he made his last confession. There were to be no consoling words of absolution for him. No last rites. He tried to stand before God without any mitigating arguments for his case. He said it how it was. It had been a long lonely passion and it was the loneliness that he couldn't stand anymore. There was only one other human being that he would have liked to speak to at this moment. It was too late even to write anything for Lorenzo. He took the pills slowly and deliberately, washing them down with the whisky. There was no despair in him at this moment. He knew that God would judge him on what he had wanted to become rather than what he had become. As the cocktail of pills and alcohol did at last what he had wanted for so long, he reached out to touch the crucifix on the confessional grill, but he never made it. He fell, catching his head on the sharp corner of the wooden shelf. Death came quickly and silently, unknown to anyone. It was a whole day before his body was found.

The bishop wanted no scandal and his body was taken away after dark for the post mortem. After that it was to be a quiet burial in a country churchyard in an unmarked grave with no public Mass for the Dead.

CHAPTER TWO

Unfaithful

… Sin is crouching at your door; it desires to have you …
(Genesis 3:7)

My unfaithfulness began in stunningly beautiful surroundings, deceptive and seductive. It happened at one of the better times in my life, not when I felt at a low ebb emotionally or physically, nor when I felt 'prayed out'. This whole experience of being unfaithful was a disintegration of my integrity and a sort of death of my wholeness, with unbelievably awful consequences.

I have tried to confront what it means objectively for me, to be gay. What it might mean for the church, as well as offering a very personal picture of what it's been like for me, and what it's like now. The unfaithfulness happened long before I'd processed what it meant and felt like to be gay. And my unfaithful involvement with another man came out of years of suppression and denial. These are not mitigating circumstances about what happened. I wouldn't even want to go down that road. To do that would just be another gross act of unfaithfulness to the other person involved in this story.

I'd met Dom whilst he was in his last year at school. Like many others he sometimes came to see me just to talk. He was intelligent, attractive and shy. I got on with him just the same as I did with many others in his year and throughout the school.

He left school and we didn't meet again until five years later when he was twenty-three. He contacted me because of some personal issues he wanted to talk about and came to see me. Before he returned to London he asked if he could join me on my holiday that year. I'd arranged to visit Venice. We met up a few times before the holiday and I found that when I was with him, my own deep loneliness, which was a constant companion, was assuaged.

I tried to bring these experiences and feelings into my prayer and put them before God. I've always believed that prayer is not so much about asking for things for oneself, but rather about a process that reveals God to me and me to myself. It's a sort of authenticating of experiences.

I'd never really been courageous in relationships. I have the capacity to get on with lots of different people, but nothing that sent shivers down my spine and made me feel more alive and more human than usual. I'd never loved passionately, maybe never unconditionally. I thought that possibly this was beginning to happen for the first time with Dom. It felt good. It felt exciting. It felt like a freeing of something. I must admit that until this relationship started I was not aware just how unalive I really was in the area of feelings.

My training in religious life and my understanding of priesthood, passed onto me under the three year strict Jesuit regime at Campion House, followed immediately by my equally tough novitiate and a further six years training, had done its job well. No particular friendships and thus no emotional bonding with anyone except God. I was a success story as far as this approach to life was concerned.

But now I felt I was becoming a more passionate soul, longing for beauty and the liberating feeling of love, whatever that meant. I describe the development of my relationship with Dom as more like ballet than anything else. It was a long slow dance towards each other, but as always for me, with a melancholy score in the background. I knew what was happening and I also knew that any dangerous liaisons would threaten everything I was about, yet at the same time I felt it might free me. But I was unsure of this freedom, not even knowing at any great depth what I wanted to be freed from. I saw this life-giving freedom bursting out of Dom and envied him. I don't think I'd ever experienced such freedom in my life at any stage, and wasn't sure what I'd do with it if I had it. My life had had the tranquillity of order and the coldness of it as well. Even before I'd joined religious life, I'd lived out my first sixteen years in a very deeply

Catholic context and I feel I skipped adolescence except for the angst, frustration and anger of it. In a sense adolescence was unspokenly not allowed.

The weeks went by leading up to the holiday in Venice and we danced closer. Though unspoken we both knew the score. Here had begun an inevitable journey which was to be for both of us ecstatic and tragic. The consequences of what we had both embarked upon could never have been imagined. It was to be the heavy price that some people have to pay. But it was to be too high a price for both of us, especially for Dom. It was a price I believe that not even God himself could have demanded.

My Catholic conscience kicked in big time and posed many complex questions. I had to ask myself how I could justify such involvement with Dom when I was not free to do so. At the same time I knew that when I was with Dom I felt alive, complete, more human and that I'd been looking for this in religious and priestly life, but had not discovered it there. As R. S. Thomas wrote in a poem about a priest at prayer:

To one kneeling down no word came.
Only the wind's song, saddening the lips
Of the grave saints, rigid in glass:
Or the dry whisper of unseen wings,
Bats, not angels, in the high roof. (*In a Country Church*)

At least with Dom, there were words, good words and lips that weren't sad. But along with all this there was an inexplicable fear in the pit of my stomach, which almost mocked me and whispered that it was all futile, destined for the bonfire of the vanities. In my quieter moments I reflected that all this should have happened when I was eighteen or twenty, not at thirty-five. It felt right; it felt wrong. I sometimes wanted to scream, to run, to die, to live life to the full.

My high ideals of priesthood seemed to be diminishing fast. It was about the death of my dreams. I'd never ever thought that I would be in this situation. I'd done all that I'd been taught. I prayed, I worked hard and tried, probably too hard, to be the perfect priest.

I remember in Venice on the first morning, after the first night that Dom and I were together. It was Sunday. I felt excited and scared. I poured a glass of red wine and went onto the balcony of the hotel room. I don't want to make this too dramatic but I remember the morning sun touching the glass and making the wine look like blood and the Venetian church bells reminded me that it could be. There were so many strange and disturbing thoughts that morning. I thought of my fellow priests in England celebrating Mass, of my elderly parents walking to Mass in that Lancashire mill town of my birth and ordination. I then thought about what I was doing. It felt like all that had been my life, my history up to now had never existed. It felt like I was wasting my substance.

Feeling complete one moment, incomplete and beyond redemption at the next, probably qualified me to visit a psychiatrist. And the mixed feelings and emotions continued after Venice.

I returned, back to my normal everyday pastoral work. School chaplain and assistant priest in the parish. It was the first week back and one evening a very distressed father whom I knew, came to see me. His baby was dying in the intensive care unit. The hospital chaplain had already baptised the child, but he wanted me to visit and give a blessing. I went with him, with deep feelings of being unworthy and inadequate. All that had happened in Venice was still reeling in my head. At the child's bedside were his mother and one set of grandparents. I began some prayers and put my hand on the child's head and silently begged heaven to come to earth for this child and his family. After a few words with the family, that felt shrill and empty, I walked home, feeling depressed and useless. The thought of packing it all in was as strong as it had ever been that night.

The following day both parents came to the door. I guessed the boy had died and they were there to talk about funeral arrangements. To my almost unbelieving ears they told me that their son was showing signs of recovery and was no longer on the life support machine. I couldn't sleep that night and wondered what God could possibly be playing at. At one level a validation of my priestly ministry, at another allowing me to feel complete, even happy with Dom.

I thought more and more about Dom and myself. It was exciting when we were together, but harsh at the centre of my being when I was on my own. I wondered whether this relationship with Dom was a big distraction from facing up to the dark spiritual experiences that people, who do embark on a journey to the centre of God, encounter. I thought of Pascal's words around this when he wrote of diversions which keep us from facing up to our spiritual desolations. I now felt as spiritually empty as I'd ever been and felt Godforsaken.

The great Jewish writer and Nobel Peace Prize winner Elie Wiesel wrote this about his Godforsakeness:

Never shall I forget
that nocturnal silence which deprived
me for all eternity, of the desire to live.
Never shall I forget those moments which
murdered my God and my soul, and turned
my dreams to dust. Never shall I forget
these things, even if I am condemned to
live as long as God himself. Never. (Elie Wiesel, *Night*)

There is no comparison of course between Wiesel's experiences in the Nazi death camps and my experiences. But each of our human hells is a very personal thing and real.

At this time in my life I did feel a nocturnal silence. My mind had stopped dancing, and certainly my dreams were in ruins. I was in a place of not knowing. I didn't know what to do. I also felt, maybe arrogantly, that there was no other person I could talk to. Dom was the closest human being in my life. He was my best friend. No one else came close. And yet when I brought all this to prayer I found my God was silent. Maybe not there at all. It would have been easier to come to the conclusion of his non-existence, but my conscience was bound. All my Catholic and priestly education spoke loudly of the wrongness of it all. My theology in this area was not as developed as it is now. All sorts of questions were in my mind. If I left the priesthood would it be apostasy? Would leaving for another human being be prostituting the sacred? Would I be condemned to eternal punishment? Was it worth all the risks and unanswered questions for a few years of pleasure and happiness?

According to the church, my love for Dom was a sick love. The acting out of this was intrinsically evil. So giving up the priesthood for Dom would basically cut me off from what had been my life since I could first remember.

I carried on almost on auto-pilot as a priest. I guess at this stage I didn't realise what an emotional and maybe even psychological and spiritual maze I was in. There seemed to be no way out that was satisfactory.

I made a decision to bring the relationship to an end. I thought then I might be at peace with my desires. We met in Oxford and I told Dom. He was devastated, angry and found my angst about the whole thing totally incomprehensible. There was the freedom Dom had and I didn't. The division between the sacred and the so-called secular did not seem to exist for him. He still went to Mass and communion and saw no great need to be constantly on his knees in confession, or privately for that matter.

I feel that if my spirituality, battered though it is, and my present understanding of theology and psychology, had been there then, the outcome might have been different.

As I drove home from Oxford that day I felt deeply sad, lonely and in all honesty that I'd probably made the wrong decision. We only met one more time in London when I, in a moment of feeble weakness, wanted to renege on my decision and try again with Dom. But the damage had been done.

I returned to my normal priestly ministry with a deep and inner sadness that actually caused physical pain. I was drinking too much and too often and feeling that everything was futile and empty. I felt I was walking in a dark dream. There was no human warmth anymore – well not at the level that I needed.

Soon after this the worst thing that could happen did. Dom took his own life in very awful circumstances. On that day the both of

us died and I regret his death on a daily basis and no amount of
therapy, love or prayer have been able to change that.

The cross is untenanted, and a cross with no God on it is a
terrible thing. A good friend of mine and a therapist has offered
me all the tools for moving on. I know what to do, but maybe
I've made a choice not to move on from these particular feelings
about Dom. The sin involved was not loving him, but entering
into it all, into another person's life and emotions whilst not
being free to do so. I had not had the courage to

> 'love honestly and openly and speak and perform creative
> words of love into the heart of another human being'
> (James Alison, *Faith beyond resentment*)

I was not able to be at ease at being loved either. Instead I chose
to go back to a way of life that didn't have a great deal of tangi-
ble love. I went back to the God of the Jesuit College, and my
novitiate, the one who was promised to be my best fried and
support. But I knew that what I was going back to was loneliness
and the resolute empty silence of God.

I'm writing this in the season of Lent and quite a few years on
since all this happened. The period that followed Dom's death
was the closest I've ever been to feeling that life wasn't worth it.
I think what is contained in the rest of this book will have more
glimmers of hope than this particular chapter. Lent begins with
ashes and ends with an untenanted cross and an empty grave.
My faith has changed since all of this. It's deeper, richer and certainly more courageous. Our faith starts with someone who is
not there, who is not where we thought he would be. It begins
with absence. The absence of God aches its shadows in mind,
heart and soul. Since Dom died I've had to let go of my old way
of believing, because it wasn't adequate and I would never have
been able to survive with that particular emergency kit, and
that's what it had become. There has been and still is a very
painful maturing of my spiritual life. For me, the death of Dom
and my own failure, having let Dom down so terminally, is now
part of my sharing in the passion and dereliction of the cross.

When the exhibition at the National Gallery 'Seeing Salvation' was on, I went to it. Of all the works of art I saw, one stood out more than the rest. It was a half life size sculpture of Christ sitting on a pillar. He is naked except for the crown of thorns. He is resting his head in his left hand. There is fear on his face. Even though his eyes are open they don't see anymore. Loaves will be left single now, children unblessed; miracles out of the question. Maybe his thoughts were on those he loved, but his body was shaking with fear. He had entered the dark night of false kisses and long shadows and feckless friends.

I feel that my experiences are about the right kind of emptiness now, and I'm still looking for love, his love, in the loneliness of things.

CHAPTER THREE

God in Dark Places

Moses approached the thick darkness, where God was
(Exodus 20:21)

I believe that we are created to need God. There is, right at the beginning of God's involvement with us, recorded in the book of Genesis, through the Exodus and the desert and the rebellions, right through to the Incarnation and the Apocalypse, a deep down need for God.

In the book of Genesis we see a friendly and accessible God pleased at what he has created. The description of God's relationship with Adam is both beautiful and moving. We are told that God walked with Adam through the garden in the cool of the evening. This 'at-easeness' with the one who is totally other than we are is profound and it is our destiny.

But then something happened to spoil it all for what seemed forever. It certainly did not feel for Adam and Eve and their descendants like the '*felix culpa*' of the *exultet*.

Adam took on God with one catastrophic act of disobedience, changing the history of God and his creation. The word obedience comes from two Latin words meaning to 'listen to'. Adam chose not to listen. After this, three distinct things happened to Adam and his partner Eve.

First of all they realised that they were naked. Up till this moment they had been comfortable with themselves and with their bodies, but no longer – shame had entered our human experience.

The second event is that they felt the need to hide from God. No more free and easy walks with the divine in the garden. Fear and guilt was now on humanity's menu.

The third was that as a result of shame and fear and guilt, anger and blame came in. Adam blames his partner Eve: 'The woman made me do it.' (Genesis 3:12)

So we have a picture that is all too familiar. We are not at ease with ourselves, with God or each other and our world. We are banished from the garden. Murder, floods, Babel follow, but also a promise to Abram.

'Do not be afraid, Abram I am your shield,
your very great reward,' (Genesis 15:1)

In this promise to humanity in its lostness and darkness we see a God who still can't help being involved with us, even though affronted by the deafness of his creation.

Of course the unfolding of salvation's history was still messy. Sodom and Gomorrah, the betraying of a brother, the testing of Abraham, desert, lots and lots of rules, prophets and songs and love poetry, threats and more threats with the last paragraph of the Old Testament promising

'See, I will send you the prophet Elijah before that great and-dreadful day of the Lord comes. He will turn the hearts of the fathers to their children, and the hearts of the children to their fathers ...' (Malachi 4:5-6)

And then the Incarnation.

When I found myself entering the unexpected darkness, or rather being eaten up by it, and when it felt like a permanent Ash Wednesday, where God seemed like the Bleak North, I was totally unprepared. For the most part during my seven years training leading to solemn vows and priesthood, it felt good. We were so busy, distracted by intellectual pursuits, compulsory sport and gardening and a very long and exhausting day, that there was little time to think on one's own, and when night came, it was a very welcome lights out at ten o'clock.

It was soon after ordination that the darkness descended. I was sent to a very tough parish in Edinburgh, where our Order has two communities. The area I worked in with three other priests, was a notoriously deprived area, but with some fantastic people. I became deeply sad and unhappy there. Typically I blamed external sources. I found the way community life was lived out was uninspiring and with little vision. We talked with each other very superficially and the warmth and fun of student community life felt a million miles away. I threw myself into constant work. But this did not really help. When I brought my feelings to prayer, I felt it was all futile, both the work and the prayer.

It was during this period that I became good friends with the Cardinal of St Andrew's and Edinburgh. I was his confessor. He was a deeply pastoral man, but I felt very inadequate to be offering spiritual advice to anyone, never mind a Cardinal. I still thought then that eminent people were somehow not inflicted with the flaws of humanity that seemed to be coming to life in me, and at one level being close to such a man made me feel even more inadequate. I felt I was living a double life and shouldn't be involved with the sacred and the spiritual. I also found I very easily got into the quite common drinking habits of some clergy – and it seemed to help a little at the beginning. I had at this stage no insight into my own reality, nor did I perceive what was really happening to me.

I went reluctantly to the psalms trying to use them as a sort of compass. But feeling very empty inside, even lost, it was like being a child again – needy, desperate, waiting to be loved, held. I was giving out constantly what in reality I didn't have. I felt abandoned to emptiness. I was twenty-five and I felt that I'd made the biggest mistake of my life by being ordained on the ninth of February 1974. It was like

... the ash of the sound of glory
... the ash of the book
... the ash of the city
... the ash of the world
... the ash of the flesh
... the ash of the mind
... the ash of the smile
(Ash Wednesday)

I've never much liked Ash Wednesday. I guess because it lasted for so many years and only in recent times have I begun to understand its dark beauty. Even though this dark beauty often makes me sad. It's the living through the pain that is part of the secret, rather than thinking through it.

The psalms reflect the darkness of God's people on the journey of a lifetime. There are feelings of absence, emptiness and abandonment. In the midst of what I was incomprehensively expressing, the psalms shouted out to me that there was some sort of spiritual basis for all this and this time this was only an intellectual conclusion. It was not something I felt. Psalm 77 was one that I kept going back to.

'I remembered you, O God and *I groaned'*. (Ps 77:3)

'You kept my eyes from closing; I was *too troubled to speak.'* (Ps 77:4)

'Has his unfailing love vanished forever?' (Ps 77:8)

The psalm ends with reference to Moses, whom I referred to at the beginning of this chapter who entered the thick darkness where God was.

I know from my theology and spirituality that the experience of darkness and emptiness is part of some people's journey. From a distance it had a sort of attractive quality to it. Reading John of the Cross, for example, was like seeing a good film. John in prison, neglected, the great escape and the courageous reform of the Carmelite life; it was inspiring. When St Francis, the founder of the Order I belong to, resigned as leader because he couldn't cope anymore, and went into the hills for the last two years of his life to contemplate and intercede, it had a radical and sweeping gesture to it and all later confirmed by God with the stigmata.

But when the dark night was mine I hated it and feared it. Not only were the goalposts of my life moved, the pitch wasn't where it was before either. Up until now I thought I was relying on God – in reality I was leaning on myself. I had become my own saviour.

I didn't realise in the middle of all this that darkness could be the harbinger of God, a God who sometimes encourages our displacement. But at the feelings level I was heading fast into despair. Everything about me seemed a sham and of him – nothing.

During this period there were two life-savers for me. One was the Welsh priest and poet R. S. Thomas, the other Gerard Manley Hopkins, Jesuit, poet mystic and depressive. Two dead priests with so much tranquillity and beauty to offer.

R. S. Thomas was the most helpful and inspiring of anything I read at the time. My reality and his seemed to connect. To know that another priest could wrestle with faith and with prayer and with God and his own humanity was a profound and sometimes moving experience. When I looked around at my fellow priests, they all seemed to be doing so well and seemed at ease with their faith and ministry. It was ironically a refreshing change to meet one who wasn't.

Even though above I refer to R. S. Thomas and Hopkins as two dead priests, I did go to listen to R. S. Thomas at the Cheltenham Literature Festival shortly before he died. He was just as I'd imagined him. Tall, gaunt, with a hint of the severe in his face and socially a man of few words, who didn't watch TV or read the newspapers, but knew humanity so thoroughly. He was in touch with the contemporary experience of God or his absence and the world's struggle for meaning; and its deep fear of personal annihilation at the end, where the possibility of nothingness pervades the modern psyche.

Some of the phrases he uses about God jump off the pages; they did then in that thick darkness and they do now in the shadowlands. Words like God as 'the bleak North', or God as 'such a fast God often not there when we get there, but always well ahead of us'. Or God as '... movement behind the curtain, glimpsed at through arid prayer. It's a rugged spirituality and a cold comfort theology.'

In his poem 'The Combat' he writes this of God:
You have no name.
We have wrestled with you all
Day, and now night approaches;
The darkness from which we emerged
Seeking and anonymous
You withdraw, leaving us nursing
Our bruises, our desolations!

I've always found Christmas a good time for me. Autumn and winter, in that order, are my favourite seasons. I've never felt the need, like quite a number of my fellow ministers of religion, to condemn the commercialisation and the razzamatazz of it all. I've felt for a long time that all of this is an attempt, albeit subconscious, for many to reach out for the divine extravagance that is incarnation.

With my life-long proclivity towards this attraction of sadness and darkness, I can quite easily look into the crib on Christmas morning and feel the almost futile desolation that awaits this child. Artists have tried to capture this mood as well. Sometimes the Christ-child is holding some straw that is cross-shaped, or someone is pointing to a distant untenanted cross. There is one very powerful painting of Mary holding the infant in her arms, but the baby looks dead, a foretaste of the piéta, where Mary holds her dead son after the crucifixion.

Looking back, and of course my journey is not yet over, it's been a privilege to walk with this divine child, experiencing the bruises and desolations. I don't want to go back there and I would never have had the courage to set out on this journey if I'd known what it entailed. But it has been strangely grace-filled and from the severed branch, there are some signs of a second spring.

There is a stunning work of art that was exhibited for some time at the Royal Academy. It's by Maurizio Cattelan. It shows Pope John Paul II struck to the ground by a meteor. As he tries to get up from under the weight of the meteor, using his staff, with the image of the crucified Christ at the top, his face reflects the agony and forsakenness of the crucified Christ. This is by no means a disrespectful work of art, but rather a metaphor for the third millennium, where individuals and whole societies struggle to discover the possibility of faith within a world where God often feels absent.

I saw the Pope recently at a Mass in St Peter's Square. He was frail, shaking both in body and voice, but with a faith built on a rock. I saw this faith reflected in the faces of the vast crowd, young and old trying to get a glimpse of this icon of hope.

Of course all of us, even popes and poets will have to return again and again to that very personal and particular poverty of mind, body, spirit, faith. We will always be searching for meaning towards that tree where the weather will always be '… nailing the appalled body that had asked to be born'. (R. S. Thomas, *Hill Christmas*)

The other lifeline was the Jesuit poet Gerard Manley Hopkins. When I was studying philosophy I had great difficulty getting my head around metaphysics. A rather wild and defiant adolescence in a Lancashire mill town with no books to read, but thankfully the cinema to escape to and then Latin, Latin, Latin for three years, did not prepare me for metaphysics. My philosophy professor wrote at the end of my first essay on metaphysics, 'Why didn't you tell me that you had understood nothing of what I'd taught you this term?' This was left outside my room on Christmas Eve afternoon! I immediately went to see him, not able to stay with his negative comments over the Christmas period and I found him to be more understanding than his written word. He read a poem by John Donne to me and asked me what I thought it meant. Of course it meant nothing – it didn't even rhyme! He persevered with me and then one day the penny dropped and I began not only to understand metaphysics, but even like it, and the metaphysical poets especially. And then I discovered Hopkins and his complicated poetry and loved it. It was a challenge. It was full of ecstasy and despair. It's a poetry inspired by the medieval Franciscan and philosopher Duns Scotus, along with the beauty of Old English and Welsh poetry. I was surprised that I took to it, though I did not understand it all by any means. Phrases like 'birds build – but not I build'; 'no but strain'; 'Time's eunuch' and 'not breed one work that wakes Mine, O thou Lord of life, sends my roots rain'.

I wake and feel the fell of dark, not day.
What hours, O what bleak hours we have spent
This night!
(G. M. Hopkins, *I wake and feel the fell of dark*)

O the mind, mind has mountains; cliffs of fall
Frightful, sheer, no-man fathomed. Hold then cheap
May who ne'er hung there.
(G. M. Hopkins, *No worst, there is none*)

These were the lifelines during my Winter's Tale. The Psalms and the two poets.

During all of this I was called up to see my provincial and his advisors. This was an official meeting. The tip of the iceberg they could see. I was drinking too much and I was disintegrating. Even though the questions they asked me had a sort of spiritual theme, I felt that therapy was on their minds.

I remember one of the questions I was asked, 'Do you say the Rosary?' I'm not quite sure they grasped what was happening. 'No', I replied, 'I don't.' 'Do you pray at all?' 'I think so, but not like I used to before.' I tried to explain that my prayer was god-forsaken. I said whatever experience of God I do have is fleeting and feels like dead of winter. I felt so inadequate trying to express my inner life with people who cared for me but didn't know me, or I them. And so it was decided that I needed therapy. I'll look at this process later in another chapter.

I feel those around did their best for me. I saw a copy of a letter to a friend of mine from my then provincial which demonstrated the complex problem of trying to work out what was happening in the inner depths of another human being. I quote from this letter:

It is an irony of God's workings that such a gifted and talented priest, should be burdened with such deep-seated and intractable problems.

The 'deep-seated' I could agree with even in the thick darkness, but I couldn't subscribe to 'intractable'. I've always believed that there is a way in for everybody including myself. God's grace is everywhere; the challenge is not to give up on letting God find us.

The whole process I now compare to the Bayeaux Tapestry. From the front it's a magnificent story, from behind a mish-

mash and messy tangle of multi-coloured threads. At this time I
was seeing my life from the tangled mess side – like everything
else. I felt that I was being unpicked, unmade as Gerard Manley
Hopkins writes:

> Thou hast bound bones and veins in me, fastened me flesh,
> And after it almost unmade.
> (*The Wreck of the Deutschland*)

Being unmade by God is about disintegration with a purpose.
It's about the deep down pain of what it means to be human. It's
about being very conscious of the bones and the veins, the tears
and the screams. It's about the flesh. It's about a feeling of homelessness, of not really belonging where you're supposed to belong.

There is a great deal of pain in the wide world outside, but in
the small world within, even more. There is a deep down meaning in everything and often death and birth, endings and beginnings are indistinguishable. The cross casts its shadow over
what we are and what we can become. As I write this today, the
Tuesday of Holy Week 2003, I've just spoken to the mother and
the brother of a twenty-three-year-old young man who has
taken his life in the garage of their home. I've known him since
he was twelve and I've been so shocked at the news. All the
writing in this chapter feels at the moment futile, empty and my
familiar anger at God resurfaces so quickly, though I detected
none of this in his mother or his brother. It's always the suffering
and the poor who proclaim the gospel to me. May Niel rest in
God's love.

The process of 'becoming' is that desire in us to bring to birth.
The silent and sometimes kicking and leaping God breaks
through from the darkness and safety of the womb crying into
our tear-stained world, vulnerable, lovable, needy.

For me part of the deep down mystery of God in dark places,
and of birth and death, is the life long attempt to reach out and
just touch him, because for many it does not happen.

Even though I like Holman Hunt's painting of 'Christ the

Light of the World' I would challenge the theology behind the picture. Hunt paints a compassionate Christ gently knocking at a door at night time. He carries a lamp. The door has no handle on it, suggesting that it is up to the person inside to open the door to salvation. But there are many, myself included, who find that no matter how much prayer we engage in, no matter how much searching, we cannot find a way to open the door. Some people die, the door apparently still shut. In the work I have been doing during the last eight years, in the field of addiction amongst the young, and generally working with a wide variety of people on the 'edge', this image of not being able to open the door and let in love, liberation and hope, is a daily experience. I have known twenty-two young people, three priests and two close friends, who have over this period taken their own lives, or who have died of an accidental overdose, or just bad 'gear'. Each time this happens I am thrown back to the earth where I belong, where I come from, to wrestle yet again with my flesh-bound spirituality and my hidden and frustrating God, nailing my questions to the untenanted cross.

This chapter is primarily for those who have tried and tried again and still feel they are on the edge. I guess the resurrection is only good news if you're dead – and there are many ways of being dead. It's about the dark veil of faith.

The lostness of our humanity at the experiential level that leads some people to despair and suicide, or to escape in drugs or alcohol or sex and power, is always on the menu. I feel in my own life that contraries meet in me. But I do believe that God is in this place and that's what the redemption is about. There is the real possibility of being able to make music, albeit an unfinished symphony, with God writing the final score.

Back just briefly to Holman Hunt's painting 'Christ the Light of the World'. If there is no handle on the outside for Christ to open and enter in, and the person on the other side is unable to open up, what then? Thank God for the New Testament.

On the evening of the first day of the week, when the disciples were together with the doors locked for fear of the Jews, Jesus came and stood amongst them … (John 20:19)

Still marked with the signs of failure, still wounded for all to see and even touch, he breaks through the closed, locked doors of our lives, doors which I have no chance of opening on my own. My journey through the thick darkness, or at least the beginnings of the way through it, began with a long lost allowing of myself to be touched by the wounded Christ. I've found him most present in others also who have experienced his redeeming darkness. This I discovered was the only way my wounded self, psyche, emotions, memories, wherever it hurts most, could be healed. Although at the beginning it felt like just being patched up. This being made whole will be a life long process, only being completed in eternity.

The gift of hope in all of this is teaching me that where humanity is most broken, others and mine, there are always God's extravagant gifts of grace and love. My God not only loves me, he likes me.

At one level, even though my life long travelling companion, darkness, still comes to tease me like it did today when I heard of Niel's death, I am still grateful that I have been taken to a place where I probably did not want to be when I was young and full of dreams. I feel that I have been given a gift to be along side others who are in the thick darkness. I feel at home here.

I spend most of my time with people on the edge. Not just the homeless and the young people on our re-hab, but with people who have become disillusioned with things spiritual and religious. People who are on the edge of church life, people who feel that being themselves is not acceptable. Priests whose lives are deeply lonely and spiritually empty who only catch glimpses of love. I now daily thank God for the darkness and the shadow of the cross. I wouldn't want it any other way.

The shadow of the bent cross
is warmer than yours. I see how the sinners
of history run in and out
at its dark doors and are not confounded'.
(R. S. Thomas, *Shadows*)

CHAPTER FOUR

'Untenanted Cross'

'If I must boast, I will boast of the things that show my weaknesses'
(Corinthians 2:3)

One of the most powerful pieces of art for me is the *Pièta*. Not just the most famous one of Michelangelo's in St Peter's, Rome, but all the others I've seen in different parts of the world. Mary holding flesh of her flesh, after the crucifixion, which she had done many times before when he was a baby, helps me now in my present ministry to those on the edge of life and church.

Every day I work with young, homeless and excluded people; younger and older people with drug and alcohol dependency; with those 'whose minds have stopped dancing' and with gay Catholics who often find no real place for them in the church; with others whose outer lives seem alright, but inside there is the unfathomable pain of their life's experiences of hurts and rejections.

I was very young when I first saw Michelangelo's *Pièta*. I was more interested in leaving St Peter's for Italian ice cream than looking at Italian art. Not so the last time I looked at it two years ago. I saw a woman holding her son, the man of sorrows and familiar with grief. She was not looking up to heaven for comfort or easy answers, but rather she gazed on the dead Christ. She had given her milk to this now dead son, 'Milk to our bread'.

Michelangelo has portrayed in the face of Mary a much younger woman than she would have been. Maybe emphasising her youthful virginity, going back to the day that Gabriel announced her incredible place in creation, when only about fourteen or fifteen years of age she changed the history of the universe forever. The body of the Christ figure, whilst well and truly dead, has been carved to present him as the perfect man.

One of the legs is in an awkward position and would suggest *rigor mortis*; the other stretches out with the foot resting on a felled, almost savagely felled, tree trunk, symbolising youth cut off in its prime, not dead, and from that trunk, new life will spring.

Another *pièta* that had a deep impact on me was the one I saw at a Benedictine monastery. This time it was not Mary holding the dead Christ, but Christ holding a dead young man. The young man's body was emaciated beyond imagining. He had died from AIDS. His body was shadowed by the Christ figure who held him. Christ also looked like he had AIDS. I've seen a crucifixion that was painted at the time of the Great Plague, and on the body of Christ are the marks of the Black Death.

He had no beauty or majesty to attract us to him,
Nothing in his appearance that we should desire him ...
... Surely he took up our infirmities and carried our sorrows...
... For he was cut off from the land of the living.
(*Isaiah 53: 2-4, 8*)

I remember as a boy kneeling before a life size crucifixion at the back of my parish church. I can't remember now exactly why I was there and why I requested of this God of mine that I might share in some of these sufferings for the good of the world. Of course, I'd no knowledge of what this meant in detail. At one level I didn't really know what I was talking about, but there was then a relationship of love between Christ and me, and at that moment it was a secret one too. Children have secrets, of course, imaginary friends and dreams. But this friend of mine was no imaginary one, he was more real than my friends in the playground. I'm not quite sure what contemporary psychology might make of this. I guess it could be interpreted as an escapism from my rather rough and tough boyhood environment, or some potential religious mania. I'm sure most who read this book will be easily able to dismiss the latter and those who know me will be able to do it absolutely.

Basically I volunteered to accept the invitation to take up the cross on a daily basis. I didn't realise that my boyhood crosses were quite manageable. But the one's that would come later were very different when the cross did kick in. I sometimes wondered if I'd make it to the end of the day, or to the end of the night.

I once tried to express some of this with a diocesan bishop in whose diocese I had started to work. He said, and I quote, 'Now laddie, keep your feet on the ground, all this spiritual stuff's alright in its place.' He didn't elaborate on where this place might be, but it did emphasise to me that there were very few 'Masters in Israel'. I couldn't find anybody who remotely had a handle on what seemed to be happening in me.

I happened to go into a recently refurbished Catholic church in Bristol, and there above the sanctuary was a neon cross; it wasn't flashing on and off, though it might well have been. There was no figure on it symbolising the victory of the resurrection, but at this point I was nowhere near any victory. The words of Mary of Magdala were more real to me then: 'They have taken my Lord away and I don't know where they have put him.' (John: 20:2) I wanted a cross tenanted. I needed my God on it or I might lose my faith and even my life.

Whilst on the subject of sacred art, it's interesting that as far back as 1935 the French artist M. A. Couturier, who was outspoken about the mediocrity of sacred art, compared it with the vitality of modern secular art. A crucifixion he was commissioned to create as an altar piece caused great controversy, even reaching the Vatican itself. It was too real, too painful to look at, far too personal, we couldn't look at our God like that. Couturier had been inspired to produce this particular crucifixion, based on the text of the suffering servant from Isaiah, quoted above.

Many modern artistic attempts at the crucifixion often have Christ displayed quite comfortably on the cross, even clothed in priestly vestments. I guess that there is so much to express about the cross that all of them do have validity. Most bishops wear a pectoral cross with no figure on it and sometimes decorated with precious stones, symbolising the resurrection and the victory of Christ over death. The English bishops seem to have a rather peculiar way of wearing their pectoral cross in public when they are just wearing a black suit and Roman collar. They place the cross in their inside jacket pocket, with just the gold chain showing!

The place where the cross casts its long shadow is the place of the most extreme testing. It's the place where atheism is conceived. I remember being in hospital for an operation on a dislocated shoulder, a very brave and gentle minister of religion came round and went to every patient. I remember one man across from me saying to him, 'No thanks, sir, it was the war that made me not believe.'

The experiences of so many people who endure unspeakable sufferings is always a deep mystery, no matter how thin the thread of faith is between a human being and his God. It remains a mystery always if there is a God. Not quite so much a mystery if there isn't one.

The great Jewish writer, whom I feel represented the conscience of the Jewish people, especially with regard to any sort of spirituality that could be gleaned from the Holocaust, is Elie Wiesel. He was fourteen when he was sent to Auschwitz. If you want 'disturbing', then read his book called *Night*. He writes in *Night*:

> Not far from us, flames were leaping up from a ditch, gigantic flames. They were burning something. A lorry drew up at the pit and delivered its load of little children. Babies! Yes, I saw it – saw it with my own eyes … these children in the flames … How could it be possible for them to burn people, children, and the world to keep silent? … Around us everybody was weeping. Someone began to recite the Kaddish, the prayer for the dead. I do not know if it has ever happened before, in the long history of the Jews, that people have ever recited the prayer for the dead for themselves … 'May his name be blessed and magnified …' whispered my father.

Wiesel goes on in the book to challenge his father's faith, along with the whole of Europe's, for not just the Pope seemed silent, but God seemed silent as well.

The chapter 'Unfaithful' I found both very difficult and yet very necessary to write about that period of my life. The next paragraphs are almost more painful to write about, but they are an integral part of my life pilgrimage. I use the word *pilgrimage* deliberately, because I believe that this is not just any old journey, aimless and without meaning. For me by using the word *pilgrimage*, it means that no matter how hidden God seems, he is integrally involved. So nothing is insignificant, and there is a deep down meaning and purpose in our experience, though we might not ever know that fully.

There was a short and despairing period in my life that nearly brought it to an end. Dom from the chapter 'Unfaithful' was dead. I was living, but not really. I woke up, or rather became conscious, to find myself miles away from home in a psychiatric ward. The first face I saw was that of a middle-aged woman whom I later became fond of. She was to be my psychiatrist for the five weeks I stayed in hospital. She told me that when I was brought in I suffered cardiac arrest and was almost lost. I only vaguely remembered overdosing. I felt so guilty and ashamed. When I began to recover I phoned a few people and it wasn't long before lots of letters and cards came in from the parish and the school and elsewhere, over 500 in all. I found them almost too painful to read.

I also wrote to the bishop whose diocese I was working in. He was a deeply pastoral and gentle man who went out of his way to support me, along with the parish priest and parishioners. The school I was chaplain to wanted me back when I was well. The psychiatrist thought this was an excellent idea too.

During the first week I was there I had visits every weekend from parishioners and families who drove over a hundred miles each way. The local priest was very good indeed, and another priest friend called often.

My own provincial at the time did not contact me either by letter or phone. It had been too long a winter for him with me, and he saw me as someone unreachable. I felt the same way – I couldn't reach the depths of me.

The day before I was due to be discharged I received a letter from my provincial. He prefaced the main part of his letter with

an intimation that this would hurt me. The bishop had expressed his views and wanted to have me back – but my provincial said 'No' and he also told me I was now completely on my
own, with no financial or other support from the order.

I now know where he was coming from. He was trying I
guess on advice from the experts to create a sort of rock bottom
experience for me, so that I might be brought to my senses. The
words of John Henry Newman were never more true than with
me:

> Pride ruled my will,
> remember not past years.
> (John Henry Newman, *Lead Kindly Light*)

Rock bottom was something that I was all too familiar with.
What confounded me and people who knew me is that I kept
resurfacing, sometimes with excess energy and enthusiasm and
creativity. But for my real healing, even conversion, I was to be
led to somewhere else. It was not counselling, or reality therapy,
which I called brain surgery with a sledge hammer, but something other that began to take me on that long pilgrimage to a
vision of wholeness – but a wholeness that I would never pos-
sess completely.

Recently I took a group of the young people on our re-hab
programme into the Anglican Cathedral in Blackburn. We
looked at three different pieces of art, all of them religious, of
course, but I asked the young people to bring to the art - themselves, using the past, the present, recovery and future hope. I
asked them to see the sculptures as spiritual works, which each
individual could receive something from and share with the rest
of us.

The first one we looked at was a wooden carving of Mary
from Africa. We sat round it and we waited for some comments.
The first person to speak said he thought that Mary looked sad.
We developed this a bit and several suggestions came forward
like, that it was carved in Africa where there were so many tribal
wars, and famine and drought, and of course a continent where
hundreds of thousands of people were dying of AIDS. It would

be difficult not to have sadness in this context. Hope? 'Yes', someone said. Her hands were clasped in prayer, eyes not looking heavenwards – but to the pained soil of Africa.

We moved on to the second sculpture. This was a half size terracotta work of art of Mary with her son. But this time, he is at the walking stage. Mary is trying to bath him, but he has one foot in the bath, the other outside, with an almost wicked smile of determination on his face. This was more challenging for the group to comment on. But we did get there. Here was a sign of hope, and danger for the world, ready to be about his Father's business. The sculptor has very interestingly given Mary two expressions on her face. Looked at on one side she is smiling, on the other, the sadness of the African Madonna. Letting this child go, letting this child in, brings a mixture of life experiences that are both redemptive and pained.

The third piece of art is the magnificent, very modern resurrection over the west door. It's larger than life and very powerful. The very first comment from one of the young people on the re-hab was, 'He's still got the holes in his hands and feet.' Of course any kind of recovery, especially in addiction to drugs, always carries with it the very real wounds. There is no cure only on-going day-at-a-time recovery. Sometimes in life people's wounds are more hidden and private, no less real, but others don't always know. Not so with addiction to drugs – it's so public eventually. The challenge is not to be astonished at the sign of pain, vulnerability and failure. After the resurrection Christ was still marked with the signs of his dereliction and passion. The moral theologian Seán Fagan SM, in his review of a book called *Christianity in Ireland* by Brendan Bradshaw and Daire Keogh writes this:

> Plain speaking about the darker side of our history should remind us that we may be closer to the gospel in failure and humiliation than in the wrong kind of power and glory.

He also goes on to say something which I feel is so important today. One of the reasons for writing this book was to offer an honest and transparent look at one man trying to live out a priesthood that is flawed with the frailties of human nature, but always has the reality of redemption at hand. Fagan writes in his review of Louise Fuller's book, *Irish Catholicism since 1950, the Undoing of a Culture,* commenting on the Church's current problems:

> ... the most potentially corrosive charge it has to face now is that of hypocrisy, of defending the indefensible. More than lawyers and spin-doctors, it needs the virtues of openness, transparency, accountability and humility.

I've noticed that when people do become more transparent, open and even vulnerable, there is a deep attractiveness about them. They are more approachable; they are more real. Of course reality hurts, but as the skin horse says to the velveteen rabbit, 'When you're real you don't mind being hurt'. (Margery Williams, *The Velveteen Rabbit*)

I believe the untenanted cross calls us to name our own darkness, to name the church's darkness and to name the world's darkness; but not to name and shame, quite the opposite. I often feel that our attempts at wholeness are destined for the 'bonfire of the vanities'. 'Doomed' is built in to the human condition like the inevitable doom one can find in a Thomas Hardy novel. We miss out on what really needs to be addressed in our attempt at popular bookshelf psychology. Modern psychology, modern life shies away from what our real destiny and purpose is all about – the spiritual. We try to live apart from God and his self-revealing story. We wear the untenanted cross around our necks as a fashion statement. We sentimentalise life, we are wooed by superstition and won't walk under ladders or cross on the stairs, in case it brings bad luck. The great life challenge is to engage with this God of ours – the Word made flesh whose body was abused and battered and laughed at, leaves us with this painful reality. We laugh at the foot of the cross, and live as if it never existed

> ... The gamblers
> at the foot of the unnoticed
> cross went on with

their dicing; yet the invisible
garment for which they played
was no longer at stake, but worn
by him in his risen existence.
(R. S. Thomas, *Suddenly*)

We are, as church, and many of us as individuals, at a cross-roads. We've been standing here now for a long time. There is a great weariness in the church. Fundamentalism does seem to flourish at this particular time in our church's history. I feel that this is partly due to a spirituality and a mysticism that has been left out of the pastoral equation. I was speaking to a friend of mine who is a bishop and he said to me he felt lost and inadequate. He said that he felt more like a manager than a shepherd. A Catholic Chicago prostitute was asked by someone doing some sort of pastoral survey, 'How do you see the church for you today?' She answered, 'I see the church as a very, very old grandmother who does not see well anymore, does not hear well anymore, and does not get out much anymore.'

A second birth is being called for, as Jesus said to Nicodemus when he told him that a man had to be born again, or a second spring as preached by Cardinal Newman. The Hebrew word for compassion is derived from the word for womb. This book, which even if it looks head on at the brokenness of the human condition, especially my own, is also a book about redemption and redemption is always about compassion.

We don't have to look far to see opportunities for this compassion, and compassion is not about feeling sorry for people or ourselves – it's about getting our hands dirty as we struggle for others who might be drowning before our very eyes, 'managed' but not 'shepherded' with pain and wounds that go to the very depths of body and spirit.

The untenanted cross is a powerful and sometimes fragmenting symbol in our midst. Here the extravagant compassion of God is demonstrated. The call for us to take up this cross is the most challenging of all our calls. It focuses us if we accept. This untenanted cross was and is becoming more and more for me a challenge to be where I am. It's a sign of redemption and of vulnerability. Each day I am able to see the cross made flesh in so many people's lives. It's an undeserved privilege and sometimes brings with it too much pain. But I now thank God for the cross in my life. My own personal life does not make sense without it.

With the cross untenanted, we meet him in so many places. In eyes not his, in pain not his, in the people of no importance, in the broken-hearted, in the seeking, in the lost, in the hopeful, in lovers, in losers and of course in our very own mind, heart and soul.

CHAPTER FIVE

Prayed Out

The tempest comes out from its chamber ... The breath of God
produces ice. (Job: 37:9, 10)

My mother was a convert to Catholicism and it was she, rather than my cradle Irish Catholic father, who taught me the beginnings of faith. I remember her guiding my hand to make the sign of the cross. I think this was the very first thing I do remember. One could never have guessed where all this was to lead.

I sometimes wonder what life would have been like without all this. Maybe wishing like some of the Indians of the rainforests of South America, fought over and killed by the Spanish and Portuguese, that the wind had not brought the ships of these men of religion into their lives.

Whenever I return to my home town, these days a rare event, and visit the church where all the sacred things of my life took place, I feel a stranger there. I see the font of my baptism, not liturgically moved from its original spot. The confessional with the same battered crucifix on the immovable grill; the faded silk purple stole; the high altar, not moved; the tabernacle still where it always was from where came my very first taste of God. The place where I lay prostrate for the Litany of the Saints on the day of my ordination and the space in the aisle where I bade farewell to my father and then my mother. It feels like I'm carrying something dead inside me and that I'm scared that someone might notice.

The red light that burns there was once a great comfort to me on some of the down days of my youth, but now it says something else. It says, nothing! What a silence in this presence!

The experience of the emptiness of things, the great 'nothing' where there was once a great 'something', takes away any illusion of being in control of one's destiny. I can't help being amused at so many book titles in the popular psychology section of every major book shop, like *How to Become the Person You Most Want to Be, Happiness – a 30 day Guide, I'm OK You're OK*, or even a retreat I saw advertised in *The Tablet*, 'Discovering God in an atmosphere of relaxation – tasting the wines of Tuscany'.

I've thought for a long time that if I should want to make God laugh, I'd tell him my plans.

During my turbulent adolescence, from about fourteen to sixteen years of age, I was saved from self-destruction and crime by a saintly and scholarly Jesuit to whom I referred in the preface. He stretched me beyond my then capabilities. He gave me books to read that didn't always make sense to me and we discussed and discovered them together. He gave me books on the lives of the saints. As always in my life there have been massive contradictions. There was I, creating havoc at home and at school whilst at the same time reading the lives of the saints.

I used to read to him because his eyesight was very poor. He eventually told me why this was. It was when he had been a boy at Stonyhurst. He and some others on the train home for the holidays had been involved in some sort of vandalism which ended up with him falling from the train and hitting his head badly, which started the process of his sight diminishing over the years. When I heard this I was even more impressed with him.

In the middle of my unacceptable behaviour, especially at home, I wanted deep down for it to stop, but I didn't know how to do it. It seemed totally out of control. But this I do know, when I was with this priest I saw that it was possible to be good.

He took me out with him during the holidays on rural pastoral visits to far flung villages and farms in the Ribble Valley. We either caught buses or he'd manage to organise a lift. He'd obviously seen in me what has taken half a lifetime for me to see. He was also the kindest of men, and the kindest of confessors. Going into confession with the common sins of adolescence never seemed to faze him. Unlike the other priests in the Jesuit community, he never asked questions. With him it was mercy freely, non-judgementally given. Mercy within mercy within mercy. It was all this, rather than what I learned as a student for the priesthood, that I eventually brought to my own priesthood. He was my first and best teacher, and even though I wandered far from all this for a while, into areas where he would never have dreamed of going, it was back to his way that my journey took me, and is still taking me. I happened to be on holiday the day he was being put into a nursing home. I went up to his room to see him. He was sitting on the end of his bed, wearing his Jesuit gown and biretta, with a very small, battered, brown, suitcase by his side. I don't think he knew who I was, yet he received me with laughter and conversation that made it clear to me that he was not really aware of what was happening. I was glad of this. He died shortly after and I travelled up north for his simple funeral. As G. K. Chesterton wrote of St Francis of Assisi when he died, I can also say about this priest: 'The world lost a good friend.' I certainly did anyway. But I was to enter a very de-stabilised world.

And those angel faces
which I have loved long since,
and lost awhile. *(John Henry Newman)*

This priest had introduced me gradually to a different way of praying, which has stayed with me, when I could pray, all my life. He taught me that primarily a priest's prayer is about inter-cession for others, rather than asking for oneself. He told me how important it was to 'hang around' God, if we wanted him to reveal himself. I felt a bit out of my depth in all of this – a feeling that went off the Richter scale in the years following ordination. Of course, then I'd no idea that God was taking me somewhere, where he wanted me to be. I didn't know then what I know now, that at the heart of God's involvement with me, there was to be a real displacement, and a journey to be with people of no import-ance, people on the edge of everything. But I had to go there first myself, before I could even begin to glimpse what was going on.

Rembrandt's powerful painting of The Prodigal Son sums up for me what being 'prayed out' is. Of all the gospel stories this one is my autobiography, and I would like to meditate with you on it.

The painting shows the end of one story and the beginning of another. The younger son at last on his knees being held in love by his long since rejected father.

But it wasn't always like that. Like the son in the story, the first part of my religious and priestly training had the security and tranquillity of order. I was summoned by bells, calling me to get up in the morning, calling me to eat, to study, to work, to play, to pray, to sleep. It seemed a good place to be for me, after the out-of-control years of adolescence. Then shortly after ordination something beyond my understanding and experience up till then began to happen. I'd been on my knees since I could first remember. Twenty-five years. I looked round my father's house and looked at my father, and didn't want to be there anymore. Had all this been a preparation for the big emptiness?

> He had no power to pray,
> his back turned on the interior
> he looked out on a universe
> that was without knowledge
> of him and kept his place
> there for an hour on that lean
> threshold, neither outside nor in.
> (R. S. Thomas, *The Porch*)

In one story of the prodigal son, the younger boy asks his father for what would come to him when his father died. In other words amongst the mixed messages of dissatisfaction, boredom, lack of excitement and just wanting to get away, the boy was also saying to his father that as far as he was concerned, his father was dead already. He was asking for the world now, only to be diminished by it. This feeling of the deadness of God is not out of the ordinary in the lives of many people. It is there in the lives of people who have spent a whole lifetime searching for him, in religious life or priestly ministry. It's an interesting fact that the only therapeutic centre specifically for clergy and religious in England is usually full all the year round. The Servants of the Paraclete who run this place offer a tremendous service to the church, even though their therapeutic methods are not for everyone.

Of course the decision of the younger son to leave home, could be interpreted as simply running away. A 'geographical', more about the illusion that being somewhere else would take away the character defects that made his life at home unbearable. It's quite common to move, thinking that things will be better somewhere else.

Wherever we go the divine seeks us out, as he did Adam in the Garden of Eden. The poet Francis Thompson describes this process vividly in his poem 'The Hound of Heaven':

I fled Him down the nights and down the days;
I fled Him down the arches of the years
I fled Him, down the labyrinthine ways
Of my own mind; and in the mist of tears
I hid from Him ...
... From those strong Feet, that followed after
But with unhurrying chase,
... and a Voice beat
More insistant than the Feet –
'All things betray thee, who betrayest Me.'

There is a great phrase in a rather poetic translation of the Prodigal Son. Jesus says of the younger son, 'He wasted his substance!' His 'isness' was on the line. And here we see a boy who was stubborn in his head and haughty in his heart.

In this poetic interpretation of the parable there are some other interesting and profound phrases. We are told that the boy travels along, 'Till at night, he came to a city', and that city was Babylon, bringing to mind all that awful unjust and pained experience for the Jewish people – the place of captivity by the rivers of Babylon, where they sat down and wept remembering Zion. It was to be a long time before the boy did the same, and remembered his father's house. It was to be a long time for me too.

The priest lies down alone
face to face with the darkness
that is the nothing from which nothing
comes. 'Love' he protest, 'love'

in spiritual copulation
with a non-body, hearing the echoes
dying away, languishing under the owl's curse.
(R. S. Thomas, *Questions*)

I think for me Babylon, and this feeling of being very much alone face to face with the darkness, was being taken to the priestly therapeutic centre to undergo a process of therapy that was more painful than I can find words to describe. It was not negotiable – I either went, or be suspended with canonical warnings. I felt bullied, and that what I did have to say about myself was not taken seriously. This experience of being a man of no importance, where words and views counted for nothing, have helped me in my current pastoral work with other people of no importance. It taught me to work alongside them with dignity, listening and doing everything within one's power to help.

It wasn't really about drinking too much, it was something deeper and more mysterious. It was about the irony of God's workings in this particular human being. But when I tried to speak along these lines, the response I got made me feel that maybe I was losing my sanity. Something was happening deep within me.

In the poetic version of the prodigal son I've referred to, it says this of the younger son:
He wasted his substance ...
In the evening, in the black and dark of night
With the sweet sinning women of Babylon
And they stripped him of his money
And they left him broke and ragged
In the streets of Babylon.

Well there weren't any 'sweet sinning women' at the therapeutic centre, but the priests who ran it had been round the block a few times themselves and I do think there was tough love at the bottom of it all. The therapy was called 'reality therapy' based on a model called the Minnesota Method. It certainly took me into an even deeper emotional darkness where there was a stripping of the emotions leading me to feel that all that had gone before was meaningless.

Some priests were there because they were involved with women, usually it seemed to me, out of deep loneliness. I became friends with one of these priests, a very well educated Cambridge graduate. A convert to Catholicism, fluent in five languages, he had helped to translate the Prayer of the Church and before ending up in therapy had been secretary to his bishop. But he had been a deeply lonely man called to be a priest, but not called to celibacy. When he came into therapy he had already become the father of a baby boy whom I eventually baptised. One day in group therapy he was given an ultimatum, never to see the women he was involved with, or the child, ever again, or leave the priesthood. He chose to leave. Unfortunately for him it didn't work out. Even though he loved his son he wasn't able to parent him.

When he died, I was invited to speak at his funeral. The new bishop had been good to him in his latter years. I was very impressed with the diocese in the way they gave a final priestly funeral, with his seventeen-year-old son serving at the Requiem Mass.

This friend of mine once told me that he was allergic to life. But the pain of loneliness in this man's life was too much for him. I don't believe for one minute that God would want this for anyone. He was a good man, who out of sheer deep down loneliness found somebody he could love, and that was the crime.

I have to say in all honesty that I did benefit from some of the therapy and still have a deep respect for the priest-psychiatrist who was in charge. But at this stage the hidden depths of me had not been touched either by myself or others. At this time I had not yet met Dom, who did touch the deeper me. It was to be something more powerful than therapy that would do this.

I've suggested in this book that God breaking through into our lives is an awesome, frightening and sometimes disconnecting experience.

And so the night will come to you
an end of vision ... the sun will set

for the prophets, the day will go black for them
… because no answer comes from God.
(Micah 3:6, 7)

Even when we are prayed out and our life is not God-centred as
it had maybe once been, the Holy Spirit of God works all the
more in us, unknown, unseen and this process of prayer, not
ours, begins to reveal the human face of God. It also begins to reveal us to ourselves at our deepest depths.

I listen
and it is you speaking
… The darkness
is the deepening shadow
of your presence: the silence a
process in the metabolism
of the being of love.
(R. S. Thomas, *Alive*)

Jesus used a most powerful phrase in the story of the prodigal
son, after speaking about this Jewish boy from a good background ending up with nothing and feeding pigs, of all animals.
Basically when he was up to his neck in it Jesus says, 'He came to
himself.' (Luke 15:17) For me this is one of the most powerful
sentences in the New Testament. Of all the journeying and travelling this young boy had been on, he now came to the very purpose of his creation, making the most difficult journey any
human being can make. He came to himself. The Self, created for
a divine purpose which if undiscovered leaves a restlessness in
us, a homelessness, a meaninglessness that has a pain and a
price beyond our imaginings. I think addiction of any kind is an
illness of meaning.

Coming to self and staring long and hard into that vera-icon
is a painful experience for most. So many memories, regrets,
missed opportunities, tears. I stayed far too long, lingering far
from where I really belonged, trying to turn my soul's darkness
into something it could never be, without being held in the long
resisted arms of God.

Half of the purpose of prayer is to come to oneself. And praying is always about waiting, and creating an empty space for God. The meaning is in the waiting. Waiting puts us in touch with a certain poverty. It's always struck me, especially working with the poor or people on the edge, as I prefer to call us, that we always have to wait.

Often the attitude behind making people wait is that they are people of no importance. I've been there often myself.

In the therapeutic centre I was sent to there was an attempt made to dismantle what had become me, and then another attempt to put me together again – not altogether successfully.

All the kings horses and all the king's men
couldn't put humpty dumpty together again!

At the time I was going through my lonely period, I must have presented myself to those with responsibility for me as an almost impossible case. Pride ruled my will and I was stubborn in my heart – traits, may I add, that I still have to work on.

But also at this time there was something serious taking place in the Order, even though it was only the English province of the Friars Minor that I was familiar with. Many were leaving, quite a number of those who had played a significant part in my religious and priestly education were going. Some to marry, to move in with a partner, female and male, some to join the Church of England so that they could marry and still exercise a ministry. There were breakdowns in health at all sorts of levels. It was a sad, even terrible, time for us all. We were all waiting to be found by something, someone, but who? Admiration has to be given to those men who, fully aware of this, were faithful and hard working in their ministry.

Truly, the therapy hadn't really worked, or as it was put to me, I hadn't worked it. And so more of the same came my way. Again and again, no matter what my protests were, I wasn't taken seriously. There was a feeling of a desperate insanity about it from those who thought that by repeating the process it might actually 'take' one day. It didn't.

I couldn't express then what was happening to me. My inner self was almost unreachable. I thought at this time that I would feel this way until I died – and the thought of waiting that long was almost intolerable.

I've never really expected happy and neat endings. After all, the image that sometimes the contemporary church shies away from is the cross where people nail their most pained questions, where lives and minds fractured by life begin to have some sort of bleak meaning, or maybe just the dark veil of faith.

The process of arriving and returning to my faith was and still is for me a long journey. To some extent the fairly extended period that followed the last dose of therapy was a good one, and yet there was something more profound needed than a worldly form of making it right again. The popular psychology section of Waterstones or any other bookshop has titles of books which I never buy, because I feel from my own experiences that it just isn't that simple, that easy. Some of the titles are basically about the individual being in charge of his own destiny. I wonder how in charge we are on the day we are due to drop dead.

Obviously, we are free to make decisions and we are responsible for those decisions. But I've found it's more about aligning one's own will with God's and this is very difficult because of human pride.

The days that followed the intensive and impersonal therapy were dark. They were both winter and spring rolled into one. I used to preside at Mass and feel totally unworthy, and sometimes as I held the Eucharistic Bread in my hands, felt no connection or bonding. I looked into the cup filled with blood red wine, the blood of the Saviour, the 'res mirablis' of the *Panis Angelicus* and saw only wine, that which had become my enemy and could destroy me completely.

I couldn't get my head round the reality. I was well again and yet there was a bleak and fathomless interior. I tried to pray and pray again, but I had no power or strength anymore to pray. Here I was called to intercede with the divine for the world, but no words came to my lips. It was a sort of 'High Noon', me with nothing to say, looking at a God who had nothing to say either.

The painting of the Prodigal Son by Rembrandt is a picture without words. No one is speaking. Here is the worn out, prayed out boy, half naked kneeling before his father with shadowy figures looking on.

We are told in the parable that whilst the boy was still a long way off, his father went out to meet him. That means of course that all the time he was on the look out for him. This is the essence of God – he goes out to meet us even when we are still a long way away.

In the painting the boy buries himself into his father's embrace. His clothes are ragged, his inner wastedness is reflected in his emaciated body. He still carries a dagger in his belt, maybe given to him by his father for safety's sake before he left home. This he hadn't sold for women or wine – he has not completely lost his identity, or forgotten where home really was. He has one sandal on and one sandal off, maybe indicating his yet unsure decision whether to stay or go and try it all again.

The hands of the father resting on the young boy's shoulders are different. One is strong and masculine, the other gentle and feminine. It's interesting that St Francis, who founded the order I belong to, suggested that the Guardians of the community (he never called them superiors) ought to be both father and mother to the rest.

I have found coming to life, allowing my mind, fractured by life, to start dancing again, to be a difficult challenge. I believe that the bottom line recovery for anyone, from anything, is to be loved back to life. It's more profound than therapy and more profound than any other way I've tried. The beginnings of my journey from 'prayed out' started with a very simple prayer given to me by a friend:

'For all that has been, thanks. For all that will be, yes.'

CHAPTER SIX

Never going to Dance Again

I will search for one my heart loves. So I looked for him but did not find him. (Song of Songs 3:3)

Generally I feel, in my own life, that it would be an illusion to see the early days with some sort of euphoric recall – longer summers, no worries or anxieties, always snow at Christmas. Obviously there were those carefree days when, as a boy of the fifties, I had a freedom in the holidays to roam and cycle wherever I wanted, even for a whole day.

There was a common poverty in post-war, working-class Britain, but I was quite unaware that we were poor. I remember my first night as a student at Campion House, Osterley, a Prep College for would be students for the priesthood, at supper with another hundred students. I didn't know why I had two knives and a side plate. I was sixteen and had never seen this before.

When I arrived at Osterley I brought with me two secrets, one known to me alone, the other just to my immediate family and the local police. To have revealed the first secret would, I feel in the sixties, have resulted in me either not being accepted for priesthood or being asked to leave immediately without discussion when found out. The second secret had a deeper impact on my psyche than I had first realised.

The first traumatic event that happened to me in my youth (my second secret) took place when I was almost twelve. I was sexually abused by a complete stranger as I walked my dog during the summer holidays. After this man had finished with me, he threw me into a large bush of nettles. Strange to say this seemed worse than the actual act of abuse itself – stung on my face and my arms and my legs.

I mention this event because it was just before my real understanding of sexuality and the terrible and sometimes intolerable reality of the discovery of my own sexual orientation – being gay was my first secret and a well-guarded one too. To be introduced to sex without love or tenderness in this way scars indelibly, and the pay back time for such a heinous act can be waited for over many years, but come it will. The sexual outrage is very deep indeed. Once when my provincial wrote to someone that my problems were deep-seated, he knew nothing of this, but his observations were correct.

My father declared this a 'subject closed'. After the police had driven me round the Ribble Valley to see if I could recognise the car which the man had been driving, I was left nursing the event, the nettles and the awful feeling that I was damaged. I was 35 years old before I told another human being about my sexuality, and this event. When all the recent sex abuse cases began to come to light, I guess I only had a glimpse of what it must have been like for those young people who had to sustain long term experiences of being 'thrown into the nettles'.

I had sad stories of my own
but they made me quiet
the way my parents failures once did.
Nobody's business
But our own, and, besides, what was left to say
These days
When the unspeakable was out there being spoken
Exhausting all sympathy?
(Stephen Dunn, *Sadness*)

Indeed the unspeakable is being spoken, but as I said in a sermon on World AIDS Day, the gay community often misses the opportunities that society does give it to speak of what it really means. Often the outward public face of being gay is presented as cheap and shallow.

I've found that part of my given ministry which I've gladly accepted is with the gay community, especially the confused and angry, and there are many Catholics I've met who feel excluded from the place they really want to belong. It has been a salutary experience.

When I saw the two-part series 'Queer as Folk' on television I felt that I would not wish that lifestyle on any young, gay person I know. It presented a way of life that was promiscuous, drug fuelled and empty. It grasped at the straws of immediate pleasure – and at a great cost. It was about a nihilism and a culture of death. It spoke of the terrible loneliness of humanity at the heart of things.

Being a priest in all of this has given me opportunities to speak of another way of finding one's place in the family of things. But like Augustine, I came to this ministry not as an innocent. I have discovered that the journey forward is to a wisdom of sorts, and wisdom is rarely innocent.

I know of one priest who is very involved in the spiritual renewal of the young in the United States, who advises that it is better to stay out of the priesthood in its present form, rather than becoming part of the problem; to stay outside in the powerless position. But I feel one can be both powerless, except for grace, and effective, in priestly ministry and always to be waiting for God to direct the way, as well as discovering the blueprint for change on the streets of our cities and towns

But, back to the issue of becoming aware of one's sexual orientation. In the early sixties in my northern Catholic world, and in my family in particular, not even 'normal sexuality' was spoken about. The main reason why I write about this aspect of my life is that I want my long pilgrimage to some sort of theological and spiritual understanding of it, to be available for others. I hope that it might be a spiritual testimony to those who are gay like me, that it might say something positive to those who don't understand, to those who condemn, and especially to the church that often contains a mixture of all these feelings.

In the great tradition of the Christian pilgrimage, I have had a series of conversion experiences – all of them totally non-spectacular. For me this seems to be an ongoing process, with God showing himself to me in often small and nondescript ways. It's a series of findings and losings, of meetings and not meeting.

... I greet him on the days
I meet him and bless when I understand
(G. M. Hopkins, *The Wreck of the Deutschland*)

To the educated secular mind, being gay is no big deal – though
this attitude is not universal by any means. But for me as I grew
into my teens in the context of a deeply Catholic family and
community almost cut off from any other realities, it was a big
deal. It became even more problematic with the desire to become a priest. I was conscious of people praying for me to be a
priest. I doubt that any of these people, including myself, could
have guessed what this priesthood would be for me.

I can't pretend that I have experienced this particular aspect
of my life as a gift or life-enhancing, at least not until more recent times, and even now it's often visited with my past Catholic
phantoms and worries. At one time in my teens I thought I'd
solved the negative feeling surrounding being gay, by intellec-
tualising it. I'd had two girl friends at the same time and that
didn't work. I'd asked God to take it away and that didn't work
– so at least I'd tried to 'get rid of it'.

One of the best books I've read recently is *Faith beyond resentment: fragments Catholic and gay* by James Alison. I found this
book powerful, prayerful and scripturally based. He describes
his experience of being a gay Catholic man as 'an unfinished
journey into discovery of being. A journey in which the Catholic
faith provides the wherewithal to make the discovery possible,
both because of and in spite of its own structure.'

This is where I gently remind the larger body of the church
that not to allow, for example, an organisation like 'Quest' for
gay Catholics, to advertise in the Catholic directory and yet fail
to provide an alternative ministry to gay people, is a scandal and
costs lives and loss of faith.

My own deep loneliness in this area lasted for too many
years, accentuated by fear. But there has been a deep down
meaning to the things that have happened, not all the time dis-
cernable on my own; scripture, poetry, theology and the love of
other people have helped reveal the deep mystery of my being.

And even though this book is called 'Prayed Out', it has been in this very process of being prayed out that I've been led to a knowing by not knowing, that has made something of the divine plan clear.

God has not only revealed something of himself to me in prayer, but has also revealed me to myself – a painful and humbling process, soul wrenching and stripping the spirit bare where one roars with the anguish of the heart. (Ps 38:9) And this prayer was usually not mine, because I was often not able to pray I thought, except in a rather arid and dark veil of faith way. It was of course the Holy Spirit praying in me, for me.

When I felt the process of my real self being shown to me and the challenge not just to lie down and wish I were dead but to set out yet again on the journey, the dance, the pilgrimage, it was, as this book indicates, after a lot of pain and emptiness. I feel that it doesn't always have to be like this, but for most who experience the need to embark on a very different and more radical movement forward, it generally is.

I think some people observing this would describe it as a mid-life crisis and maybe it is. But it's also a process of trying to make sense of it all, and to do something about it. It's all well and good knowing this intellectually, but it's making that first step into the 'now' that is important.

All my life the idea of goodness and perfection has always been very much at the forefront of my thinking. As a child I remember trying to be good in order to please my parents, but it wasn't too long before I realised that I could never really please them and I found being 'bad' much easier. It's taken me so many years to clock on to the reality that the God I have tried to get glimpses of not only loves me, but also likes me. He is the same God of the Prodigal Son who, whilst I was such a long way from home, came out to meet me.

He came out to meet a very confused and pained human being, who hadn't the guts to be faithful, either to priesthood or to another human being and, instead of throwing myself into the arms of the living God, chose a path of self-destruction at so many levels. I tried to kill the pain with alcohol. I feel that if this divine movement towards me had not taken place, I might never have made it at all to my rather imperfect present.

Mary Oliver writes that 'you do not have to walk on your knees/for a hundred miles through the desert.' This is what I'd chosen to do – or rather had been reduced to. The experience of course eventually brought me, willingly yet desperately, to my knees.

And so long as you have not known
This: to die and so to grow,
You are only a troubled guest
On the dark earth.
(Johann Wolfgang von Goethe, *The Holy Longing*)

I looked at myself in a hypothetical mirror and saw nothing worth saving – and anyway saving for what?

Dom was dead and my priesthood and humanity felt the same way. Now I found the challenge to let the real me, sexuality and all, either keep me bound as a human being, with nothing but guilt for the past, anxiety and worry for the present and with no real hope for the future, or risk and take unknown steps. There was an anger in me and I knew that there were various ways of dealing with this. But one thing I did take on board from my visits to the priestly therapeutic centre was that anger and resentment were luxuries that this individual could not safely afford to have. They would lead me back to self-pity, self-loathing and the desperate escape into oblivion.

How could I let 'the soft animal of my body love what it loves' – it all seemed to go against the grain of what my spiritual formation was all about. I had loved in this way in the past, but my conscience bound with so much of my past, 'guilty of dust and sin' (John Donne) seemed to hold me back. I kept hoping that the official, teaching church which I love and respect, would say something positive about me and other people like me. I failed at this particular period in my life to see that God who is for sure present in his church, is not confined to it. There were other voices speaking to me, although I did not hear them well.

These were voices that actually valued what I claim to call my rather battered self and priesthood. And God of course, as is his way, was working in all of this and telling me as I know now, to waken to what those people were saying about my ministry and how they valued it. Quite a number of course knew 'about me' and still wanted me to conduct the major sacramental milestones of their lives, and found me an understanding confessor. The more astute, of course, guessed I must have been somewhere dark to be this way.

But my Catholic upbringing kept me looking beyond the Alps for answers. But even now, the very day I am writing this, there are still very mixed church messages. I have before me the 13 September 03 copy of *The Tablet* with a piece that does have a glimmer of hope in it, entitled 'Cardinal refuses to forbid gay Masses'. This is about the monthly celebration of Mass for gay people at St Ann's Church in Soho. To be fair, the Vatican did issue a statement on the pastoral care of homosexuals, saying that it recognised the need to provide 'at all levels, through sacraments, through prayers, witness counsel and individual care' a pastoral ministry to gay people.

But the opponents to all of this said that they could not imagine that adulterous or promiscuous men would be singled out and indulged even if they felt compelled to act as they did. Also from the same opponents came statements like 'Homosexuals like all sinners properly receive pastoral care in confession' – if only. Another critic likened '… the Masses at St Ann's to giving special care to extreme groups like the National Front.' I feel that many of these people would be happy if gay people did not exist at all, even if they lived a free life choice of celibacy. Thank God there is no 'final solution', to recall one man's attempt to deal with this within living memory.

I know that the gay activists like Peter Tatchell take quite extreme and angry actions to this sort of stuff like 'naming and shaming', especially people in authority both secular and religious. He once climbed into the pulpit at Canterbury Cathedral whilst the archbishop was preaching, and on another occasion let off helium filled condoms in Westminster Cathedral.

The way forward for me was to see that no matter what others said, there was a divine hand in this aspect of my life. And so I told God of my despair and waited for him to tell me his, and to my surprise he did.

> There are nights that are so still
> that I can hear the small owl calling
> far off and a fox barking
> miles away. It is then that I lie
> in the lean hours awake listening
> to the swell born somewhere in the Atlantic
> rising and falling, rising and falling
> wave on wave on the lazy shore
> by the village, that is without light
> and companionless. And the thought comes
> of that other being who is awake, too,
> letting our prayers break on him,
> not like this for a few hours,
> but for days, years, for eternity.'
> (R. S. Thomas, *The Others*)

It was only then when I knew something of the despair of God, something of the meaning of the cross, somehow new again for me, that I could move from my cold and frozen self, where almost everything about me had shut down. It was like my whole past was being dealt with – not that it all made sense, but there was the certainty of faith that no matter who I was, or what I had been involved in, there was a God, my God, who could handle it, the same God who looked out on creation at the beginning and saw that it was good. And the same God who looked out at it again from the cross and saw that it was worth saving. I had taken the first step of my journey out of darkness. It was about stripping the spirit bare.

Maybe this is why I've always considered autumn as my favourite season. I like the colours, the smells, the mists, the darkness of both morning and evening. I like the smell of the burning of the leaves. Decomposition and death in nature is quite beautiful. Now with God speaking to me of despair I had the courage to set about what the poet Laurence Binyon wrote about:

> Now is the time for stripping the spirit bare,
> Time for the burning of days ended and done,
> Idle solace of things that have gone before;
> Rootless hope and fruitless desire are there;
> Let them go to the fire, with never a look back;
> The world that was ours is a world that is ours no more.
> (Laurence Binyon, *The Burning of the Leaves*)

My entering into this process of self-discovery and getting rid of things that bound me and had stopped me developing, and throwing them onto the bonfire of the vanities, was a painful one. I had for too long been carrying around with me the excess baggage of my past. It was fine to burn the 'days ended and done'. There were of course certain things that I did not want to burn because they could never be ended and done. Dom, from the chapter 'Unfaithful', was the first and foremost someone I wanted to think about, and feel for, every day of my life. The fact that he was gone could not be burnt into ashes, even though his body had been, but it could become something life-enhancing.

The unbinding process came about by so many other people who loved and cared for me. One person in particular became my closest and best friend – this friendship is now in its tenth year and still growing and changing, but what doesn't change is the underlying love and care that we have for each other, a pure love that often challenges but always encourages growth. Many families up and down the country, and young people I worked with in their teens, who are now in their thirties, show a friend-ship and a love that I didn't think would endure. But I have found that in general their capacity for faithfulness is stronger than mine and all of this when they were aware of my story – a story which I once was deeply ashamed of, when the only energy in my life seemed to be a death energy; when I actually believed the voices around and within me that said I was not only unwor-thy, which in fact I can still happily take on board, but of no real value because whatever it was that was happening in me was 'intractable,' to use a word of one of my provincials. No way in and no way out – unless by my own hand. The fact that I did contemplate this on more than one occasion caused me a lot of worry and guilt – until I discovered this from Aeldred of Rievaulx:

> Terrible was the distress I felt within myself, tormenting and corrupting my soul with intolerable stench. And unless you had quickly stretched out your hand, not being able to tolerate myself, I might have taken the most desperate remedy of despair.

Because of what I know was happening too often within the gay community, I trained with Gloucester Friend, a help line and be-friending and counselling service for gay people. I am now a member of Lancashire Friend. Too many young, gay people and older people were in deep distress and experiencing deep loneliness and isolation about their sexuality. Some took their lives. There was no way that I, as a gay man and priest and a follower of St Francis, could not be there in some sort of loving service. These people have done so much for me, and being in their company is often life enhancing in a sometimes lonely and hostile world. But I'd also realised in all of this that my life is not primarily about me. I am only a passing fragment of something much bigger than me. Where I thought I was bringing something of the blessings of God to the 'church isolated' and often 'society isolated' gay community, I received a greater blessing in return.

I can name this blessing as a sort of reclaiming of Christian friendship. I have felt more accepted, totally non-judged and even loved, than anywhere else where I'd belonged; and all of this often in the context of a wounded and vulnerable community.

> Faithful are the words of a friend;
> profuse are the kisses of an enemy. (Proverbs 27:6)

This acceptance and love has also challenged and purified me in the fire of truth, where sometimes my real friends have told me in no uncertain terms, 'It's not good for you to do that.' This holding up of mirrors to each other is a real prophetic ministry and very dear friends do this. Aeldred has a beautiful sentence which says: 'Here we are, you and I, and I hope a third, Christ, in our midst.'

For me to be loved back to life and dignity, tough though the process is, allows me to stand before my God just as I am, not quite sure of all the 'whys' of my being and not always clear of the deep down plan for me. Always becoming , never fully arriving and never fully knowing. And even when discovering something of love and belonging there are still deep down questions which I feel will always be there for me. Of course there are still the dark days and weeks and my particular ministry on the edges of things takes me down bleak roads often. Some days as I try to sustain my spiritual life, with service to others and the beauty of the words and music of evensong in Blackburn Anglican Cathedral, I still ask what must seem too bleak a question of myself:

... Is there a place
here for the spirit? Is there time
on this brief platform for anything
other than mind's failure to explain itself?
(R. S. Thomas, *Balance*)

In the last part of the poem 'Wild Geese', Mary Oliver writes about 'heading home again'. I feel I'd like to express it by saying 'heading home, again and again and again'. When T. S. Eliot wrote of journey he spoke of the experience of finding ourselves back where we started from, recognising it for the first time.

The going home process for me is a little illusory. Several times in my life I thought I'd discovered 'home' – religious life, priesthood, Dom, a new type of ministry – but all of these have proved to be just brief visits, glimpses of what I imagine 'home' to be. Dom was probably the only one who could have been a cornerstone in such a home. But those years ago I was unskilled in building and, like the three little pigs, built on unsure foundations, and there were plenty of people with strong breaths to blow them down – including my own Catholic conscience.

I feel that 'home' for me is the home of a rather restless wanderer, a tent dweller always moving not so much to the certainties of God's presence, but rather towards the possibility of presence. This certainty makes the pilgrimage more exciting because I know if I am seeing right, his presence, his grace, his love is everywhere, waiting to be discovered, and acknowledged, some times for the first time.

The remarkable thing for me is the power of his presence in places and people, where I did not expect to find him, and at the same time not experiencing this presence in the familiar places, where my faith certainly assures me of this presence, but it does not ignite me at my deepest depths.

The poem 'Wild Geese' ends with powerful affirmation, where the world calls to us like the wild geese on their journey home, harsh and exciting, telling us of our value and place in creation – whoever we are.

Part of finding my place in creation and knowing that God not only loves me, but likes me just as I am, has been a sometimes harsh, but exciting experience. All the things about me that I felt ashamed of, guilty about, are the places where God has chosen to meet me. It's almost sacramental like the washing of feet, where he chooses to touch me in these sometimes dark and damaged places, worn out and tired after a lot of miles heading in the wrong direction. Wherever home is, I'm not quite sure. I gladly now greet my God on those days when I get a glimpse of his presence, a clue that at least he's been there. A hand of affection on my shoulder from someone with nothing else to give but that; the beauty of the psalms in a cathedral not my own; it doesn't always have a logic to it, but it does have a meaning, and I bless when I understand and see a little of the divine through the living icons of the people who are a daily part of my life, and people of all my days who have been part of it.

Now is the time to dance – a little.

CHAPTER SEVEN

No Greater Love – Amazed by Freindship

For to see your face is like seeing the face of God.
(Genesis 33:10)

I'm just looking through the programme of events at a popular 'Spirituality Centre' here in England. The topics available are interesting and sometimes mildly amusing.

Sacred Touch – a workshop for women considering the importance of the touch of God and human touch in the healthy development of body and spirit. Massage will be offered.

Heaven and Earth – a retreat for those who find God in gardens whether sitting in contemplative enjoyment or pruning, planting or playing.

God of the Senses – a retreat integrating body, mind and spirit.

Come then Beloved – a retreat for women whatever their sexual orientation, to explore issues of sexuality, intimacy and bodiliness in a prayerful context.

I mention all of the above to demonstrate the radical change of emphasis in contemporary approaches to spirituality and discernment, whether one thinks it's a good thing or not.

Personally I admire any creative input into spirituality and the journey towards God in general. My only criticism is that it's not too available for the low waged and those we might, sometimes wrongly, think wouldn't appreciate it anyway.

I know at T.H.O.M.A.S. where I work (T.H.O.M.A.S. by the way stand for 'Those on the Margins of a Society') when the recovery spirituality part of the programme is offered to the young addicts on our re-hab, it opens up powerful pathways into recovery. This, alongside a synthesis of a Twelve Steps programme and an eclectic programme to support recovery, is basically about a spiritual experience. We have a White Board right at the heart of our home with *Thought for The Day* written on it. Anyone can contribute and I'm quite amazed and moved by some of the words written on there, like 'Just for today I'll be grateful', or 'Just for today I'll be me', or 'You can take a horse to the water but you can't make it think!', along with a few unprintable ones.

The spiritual journey from anywhere to anything, or from anybody to somebody, is important for every human person, whether it be from addiction to being clean, or from loneliness to belonging, from lostness to being found, or from lust to love and friendship. To break through to what is real is usually a long process as Roger Housden writes in his commentary on 'ten poems to change your life':

The soul wants heart knowledge, a felt sense of the truth, that we register not just with the mind, but with the body – with our whole being.

To discover what real friendship was all about was for me like the man in the gospel who discovered a treasure hidden in a field. It involved selling everything I had, to buy the field.

At school I had mates, but friends were more difficult to define. Nobody from my boyhood years is my close friend – I guess leaving home at sixteen and never really belonging there anymore was part of the reason. And then of course the spirituality of the 1960s was a million light years away from the sort of spirituality I mention above in one of our popular retreat centres. In fact, any particular friendships were discouraged. At Campion House, Osterly, a pre-seminary college, every month the Osterly Memorandum was read out in the refectory to emphasise the basic ground rules for survival at the college. One of the rules I remember went like this. 'At Campion House there must be no physical contact between students except on the football pitch but then only when absolutely necessary!' Needless to say we didn't play rugby! I remember one incident when a student touched the Jesuit superior on the shoulder in order to get his attention. The superior's reaction to this was one of outrage – one would have thought that a leper had kissed him on the lips.

I remember during my time at the college becoming emotionally close to someone my own age, seventeen. The feelings
were good, in fact up until then these were the deepest feelings I
had ever had. There was no question of sex, that would have
ruined it, but I was breaking the rules, which would become
more and more of a pattern for me. And part of this pattern had
already to some extent been part of my early adolescence – secrets,
lies with the underlying feeling of fear. My heart sank only yes-
terday, just for a while, when a certain Anglican bishop said gay
people ought to seek medical attention. I feel that many people
both within and outside the gay community are sick and tired
and ashamed at the way some eminent churchmen speak about
people who are gay. No one can grow alone. We are what our relationships enable us to be and we do not need cold words, especially from the church, which I believe sometimes drives people
over the edge.

The Word made flesh is no cold word of God. I feel we need a
deeper love and kindness within us.

'When we have totally surrendered to that beauty we shall be
a mighty kindness.' *(Rumi)*

I remember a conversation with a younger member of our order
about why so many were leaving, and he said that he felt we
were suffering from deep lovelessness. I feel I've come to a stage
where I don't want lovelessness and loneliness. Part of the reason for writing this book is to say just that.

I was speaking to a friend very recently, about some of the
young people who work on the telephone line here at
Lancashire Friend, as I do, being there for people questioning
their sexuality etc. All of them at twenty seem more at ease with
themselves, including their sexuality, than I do at fifty-five. I've
only recently realised that I've a long way to come from.

As with many important developments in my life, this journey to 'amazement' and friendship with all things, has come to
me through varied and unexpected people and experiences.

It's more than obvious to anyone reading this book, that
poetry has been a life-saver and a life-giver, saving me from

what I thought my lot was going to be, a bleak life with not many laughs. I can't deny there has been deep bleakness and a sort of gallows laughter, a sort of laughter at the foot of the cross!

The ministry I'm involved with for the most part these days is 'foot of the cross' ministry, working alongside people who are on the edge of life, like myself, and it's totally amazing and life enhancing.

I think that if I'd remained in the more traditional way of living out my so called 'religious community life' I would have died, certainly inside anyway. And all the varied, mysterious, painful even sinful roads that I've found myself on have been taking me to 'here'. I don't always even remotely know what 'here' is, but it's all I've got; it sometimes feels great, at other times scary. I've found that there is a deep down meaning in everything. This foot of the cross ministry is shared with a team, not quite a community, but better than a community in my opinion, of so many people who know what the cross is all about, even those who couldn't articulate this into a theology or spirituality.

Those who lead the therapeutic part of our life are recovering from addiction themselves, and offer such deep hope for broken humanity. Some of our young team have been through the mill at other levels, some of our older team members, know the pain and loneliness of losing their life partners. We are one big dysfunctional family just wondering often how on earth all that is happening for the good, is happening, led by the founder of T.H.O.M.A.S. – a priest with a difference, who I'm sure knows what being on the 'edge' experience in his own private way is about.

Since our church was arsoned three years ago, the Blessed Sacrament has joined our dysfunctional family and resides in the house, where recently there have been considerable refurbishments, and the only place that could be found for the Blessed Sacrament was the broom cupboard on the floor. At first I thought it a bit irreverent, and then a whole glut of scripture came to mind concerning the nature of presence, of love, service and I thought of what Thomas Aquinas wrote: 'Panis Angelicus, O Res mirabilis'. The *res mirabilis* – this most wonderful thing is not just the sacrament, but human lives who often find themselves on the floor, face down, wanting to be lifted up to where they really belong.

And then we have the mostly young people, with all that goes with addiction and the illness of meaning at the heart of why we exist at all.

The theology and spirituality behind all of this for me is a strong one. I've always believed that the first announcers of the gospel, and often the best, are those whose lives have been on the edge. It is not without meaning for me that the first person to announce the resurrection was what the tradition regarded as the former prostitute, Mary Magdalene. And along side this there is always that rare certainty of God's presence in the poor, the broken, the confused, the lost. If we want to be where God is for certain, based on the scriptures, then we need to be here with them, or at least in the vicinity. Maybe we also need to be in touch with our own poverty and neediness to know that he is there too. Those on the edges of life and the eucharist are intimately, in fact I believe inseparably, connected.

It's not unusual in our house to be asked for a hug from one of the clients on that tough road to recovery. I can't ever remember once being asked for such a hug in my regular religious community life. Rather, as I've written above, we were not expected to connect physically at all.

There is amongst our client group, as the therapy progresses, a chance for meaning and happiness again, or maybe to step out into the world as if seeing it for the first time. I came across a very simple yet beautiful poem called 'Happiness'. It expresses something of the experience of recovery. When I look at all this going on around me, only a hug away, I know I'm blessed and it is then more than at other times that I want to bring this blessedness before God. It's this experience in my life that gives the beauty of the music at evensong in the cathedral an even deeper meaning and beauty. I see the faces of these young people alongside the words of scripture sung by the choir: 'The Almighty works marvels for me … He raises the lowly.' (Luke 1: 49, 52)

I also see the faces of those who are still in the grip of their struggle and pain, the ones who come to our drop-in every day, not ready yet for whatever reason to embark on that difficult journey home to meaning. I know what this feels like, and at the end of the day I don't want to be anywhere else except here. This is where I belong. I once described my ministry as a ministry amongst the ruins. I don't quite see it that way now, rather I would describe it as a ministry to the mystery of Christ's presence.

Christ plays in ten thousand places,
lovely in limbs and lovely in eyes not his!
(Gerard Manley Hopkins, *As Kingfishers Catch Fire*)

If anything can bring happiness and amazement it's this. The poem 'Happiness'says it so well and so simply for me.

So early it's still almost dark out.
I'm near the window with coffee,
and the usual early morning stuff
that passes for thought.
When I see a boy and his friend
Walking up the road
to deliver the newspaper.
They wear caps and sweaters,
and one boy has a bag over his shoulder.
They are so happy
they aren't saying anything these boys.
I think if they could, they would take
each other's arm.
It's early morning
and they are doing this thing together.
They come on slowly.
The sky is taking on light,
though the moon still hangs pale over the water.
Such beauty that for a minute

death and ambition, even love,
doesn't enter into this.
Happiness. It comes on
unexpectedly. And goes beyond, really,
any early morning talk about it!
(Raymond Carver, *Happiness*)

Like the poet, this hint of happiness that creeps into my life these days does so whilst '... it's still almost dark out!' I feel for me that this 'dark' will always be close by. A young colleague of mine at T.H.O.M.A.S. compiled an anthology of ten poems which he kindly and knowingly dedicated to me. It's called 'Ten Shades of Dark'. In the chapter 'Never Going to Dance Again' I referred to 'stripping the spirit bare'; any sort of stripping leaves one vulnerable, which of course means wounded, and this journey that I'm on with the rest of humanity is to the centre of self where the kingdom of God is. I feel that I probably ask fewer and fewer questions these days, but maintain rather a sort of incomplete, yet reasonably contented silence, like the two boys in the poem '... they aren't saying anything these boys'. Where before I seemed to do battle with God, now it's about letting go, but still feeling in my depths an ache. I'm not sure that I know fully what this ache is all about. As in the poem, 'Happiness' does come on unexpectedly, but for me leaves unexpectedly too. I'm more prone to tears these days, private mostly, and they seem to be tears from a long time ago.

There is also what I call the comfort of strangers. There are people who wander into my life, and I into theirs. Often I've found that these brief encounters on trains, or at social gatherings can open up possibilities. I do seem to have a capacity for friendship, or maybe a need for it. I also know that in my job one tends to have to let go of friends, especially when they discover they are in love with someone. I have obviously to let the new relationship grow. I found it interesting on reading a recent biography of Cardinal Newman to discover how difficult this process of letting friends go was for him. He even got quite angry when members of his close circle of male friends announced their engagements. It was not unusual for him to cut off contact after they married. I do understand this a little.

I guess at the bottom of it all is the fear of being, not alone – that's fine when one chooses it – but lonely which is not too pleasant at all. There is an existential loneliness about the human condition and the Book of Genesis advises us that it's not good for us to be alone. But as R. S. Thomas writes:

A pen appeared, and God said:
'Write what it is to be
man' ... and I spelled out
the word 'lonely'. And my hand moved
to erase it; but the voices
of all those waiting at life's
window cried out loud: 'It is true.'
(R. S. Thomas, *The Word*)

I think that the God process in my life has been eventually leading me to the very edges of my own resources, emotionally, spiritually and psychologically; a whole series of comings, of farewells to things, and an apparent taking away from me of so many things has led this reluctant pilgrim to that place where I have to rely on God. Part of this journey to friendship has been a new way of knowing God as a friend. I've resisted this close friendship for a long time. I much preferred a God who kept his distance and did not interfere too much in my daily life.

It's a strange friendship. It haunts rather than comforts. I much prefer to be held by another human being than to fall into the hands of the living God. He still seems to play games with me and peevishly seems to not want to talk, even want to play at all on some days, many days. And then all of a sudden he jumps out laughing and I forget myself for a while and he touches me. This hide and seek God can be frustrating in the extreme. He both hides and seeks at the same time, it seems. I've travelled thousands of spiritual miles looking for him but have for the most part only gleaned clues that he's been around. I ask myself why do I still want him as my friend. The fruit of my prayer has yielded a poor harvest. All these years on my knees and still he feels a stranger, and cold and warm at the same time leading me through often meaningless prayer to his bleak presence.

The broken bread of the eucharist in my sin-stained hands, and the blood poured out for all in which I can see my face, full of awe and doubt, wonder and amazement, mixed with fear of the Lord which does not feel like the beginning of wisdom, all come rushing into my mind. I think the 'ache' I referred to above is part of this real desire to want to feel like I do about a few human beings, the indescribable feeling of being in love with someone. But I've never yet experienced this with my God, no matter how often or how long I've spent in his presence in prayer.

He kneeled down
dismissing his orisons
as inappropriate …
… He fell back
on an old prayer: Teach me to know
what to pray for
He listened: After the weather of
his asking, no still, small
voice, only the parade
of ghosts, casualties
of his past intercessions. He
held out his hands, cupped
as though to receive blood, leaking
from life's side. They
remained dry as his mouth
did. But the prayer formed:
Deliver me from the long draught
Of the mind. Let leaves
from the deciduous Cross
fall on us, washing
us clean, turning our autumn
to gold by the affluence of their fountain!
(R. S. Thomas, *The Prayer*)

Why there is a resistance in me to the intimate God-friendship where my autumn could be turned to gold, I'm not quite sure.

I do know that his presence in the lives of all the people around me is a real presence. I do have deep feelings about these presences. I feel at home with his presence in the 'on the edge' people, the little ones of this world, where I feel sometimes when I reflect and meditate that there is a million light years between them and, say, the more official side of the church.

I remember visiting Venice not too long ago and seeing an old lady sitting with her back leaning against the apostolic palace of the Patriarch of Venice. She was selling postcards depicting the worst in Catholic art, just a few feet away through the walls of the palace where hang Carravagios and Tinterettos. I wondered what on earth connected her with all that went on through the other side of those walls. I guess when she put out her gnarled hands to receive the bread of life, maybe from the more privileged hands of the Cardinal Patriarch, that was the connection – a God who loved her and the Patriarch equally. But for me one spoke more powerfully of God than the other.

I also remember when I was parish priest of a very tough parish in Scotland, being called out one evening by the hard ringing of the doorbell. The boy at the door said he couldn't waken his mother. I knew the boy – he'd been confirmed that year by the Cardinal. His mother was a prostitute and an alcoholic with five children, one in prison for murder. I took the Blessed Sacrament with me and off we went, all three of us. The other three children were there. The TV was belting out one of the soaps and in a bed downstairs was their mother. The room, the house, was a mess, by the bed were some empty McEwans Export cans and an empty vodka bottle. There was a plastic bucket by the bed with vomit and excrement and cigarette ends in it. After a 999 call, I cleared a small place to put the Blessed Sacrament on. A quite black thought ran through my mind when I considered the liturgical instructions in the book I was carrying – the priest should be met at the door with someone carrying a lighted candle, and another instruction 'here a hymn maybe sung'. I called her children round and we said the Our Father and the Hail Mary and then I anointed her. She never regained consciousness and couldn't receive the living Christ in the eucharist. I broke the wafer and offered it to her children, who had all made their first communion, to receive on her behalf, with the noise of the TV soap 'Eastenders' in the background and the smell, not of incense, but of urine, alcohol and vomit. *Panis Angelicus, O res mirabilis.*

She died later that night. I remember walking home and feeling the deep pity of things where an hour before the sacramental presence of the Son of God was inches away from a woman worn out, fractured by life. It is the irony of God's workings that this woman was not able to receive the sacrament, but God had visited her home that night, summoned by a child into the broken chaos of one human life.

The 'here' where I am, which is always a challenging place to be, is where I want to be. Never now could I live a sort of secure life. It's the uncertainty of each day that fuels my energy level and, as I go to my prayer and to the celebration of the eucharist, I have so many faces before my eyes and have the pain and ache of doubt and sometimes hopelessness in my heart, alongside a faith, albeit with a dark veil, underpinning everything.

And so the journey to friendship, the journey away from hurt to the amazement of this Word Made Flesh God of mine is an exciting one. It is a lot of the time groping through shadows and with hungry ghosts from the past telling me that there is a futility about this journey. Trying to be at one with others, to see good first of all rather than anything negative, is quite challenging. Why I feel so frustrated with God is more complex. Obviously I need him as my Saviour and Redeemer – this is a need, but I want him as a friend and I will not give up on this quest.

Considering where I've been, where I've come from on this journey is amazing to me and brings a gratitude for it, but I guess I want more of God's time. Yes I've had a long way to come from, and I've still got a long way to go.

... He is such a fast
God, always before us and
Leaving as we arrive!
(R. S. Thomas, *Pilgrimages*)

How far is it to God? How far is it to the friendship that my soul longs for? Maybe not as far as I sometimes think. Maybe only a friend away.

CHAPTER EIGHT

Attentiveness – The Heart of Prayer – Out or In

'My lover spoke to me. Arise my love. and come with me, the winter is
past; the rains are over and gone ... the season of singing has come!'
(Song of Songs 2:10-12)

The ministry of 'listening' is a powerful one in contemporary counselling. One of the most successful twenty-four-hours-a-day services in this country is the Samaritans, whose main task is to listen. Before we have anything useful to say to anybody there has to be attentiveness to the other person. Cardinal Hume said in a talk on prayer, 'Safe in the market place, because at home in the desert.'

The cry of the heart in contemporary society is a cry to be heard. I found an interesting article in *The Tablet* recently about a programme of initiation of young men as part of their life journey and their spiritual survival. Its creator is an American Franciscan called Richard Rohr. It's part of trying to save young males especially from themselves and from being forever discontented and continually feeding their egos. Rohr believes women do not need such an initiation, because menstruation and childbirth save them from believing in the illusion of power.

The ego-fuelled and discontented young males should not surprise us with their behaviour of self-destruction and their death energy. Rohr believes that the reason why so many British males drink themselves into oblivion every Friday and Saturday night is because all they have is an overstretched understanding of their ego, of their self, with no knowledge of who they are in God. This road to self-destruction and violence, because of a rage inside the soul, is a road that is almost understandable.

This experience of rage was one of my early experiences. It began to show itself with the onset of adolescence. The objects of my rage of course were my parents, and later myself. I've always had a high energy level which others around me always wanted to curb or quieten down. My mind has always been active and alive, easily frustrated if the opportunity for creativity was not there. I feel I think not so much in details, like crossing the 't's or dotting the 'i's but rather in wide sweeps of sometimes vibrant colours. I found philosophy a difficult subject, logic almost unbearable and it was only when let loose into metaphysics and then theology that my thinking was challenged in a positive way. My mother described me to my headmaster, after some criminal activity involving fireworks, as a restless boy. She didn't save me from a caning but for me, in those arrogant, angry days of adolescence, that was a small price to pay and was almost a notch on the 'street cred' card of my particular small disruptive group.

This particular incident all came flooding back as I stood by my father's hospital bed shortly before he died. Next to him in a cot-type bed was my former headmaster, dribbling and crying like a child. I remembered the cane coming down onto my hands and him saying 'and you an altar boy'.

Having this restless nature was a disadvantage at trying to experience the desert in prayer. Of course the desert experience orchestrated by my novitiate and student training did help me, but the real desert, which I seem destined to spend a long time in, was far more ferocious. I felt that whatever it was that was happening to me at the core of my being was a process of being raised up to more than I could be. I felt and still do feel that in the public forum of my life, there is far less to me than meets the eye.

I've always found it almost incomprehensible to take on board the certainty of belief in many people I've met over the years. One of the most painful and challenging experiences of my life was when I was assistant priest in a parish in Cheltenham and chaplain to a local Catholic high school. My colleague and parish priest had become a member of the Neo-Catechumenate movement and was promoting it in the parish. The NC movement began in Spain under the direction of Kiko

Arquello who had rediscovered his faith and developed a form
of catechesis based on the Pauline tradition. The people who re-
sponded to the programme of catechesis in our parish were
good people who wanted to lead contemporary society back to
Christianity, developing a 'Way' of faith directed to re-discover-
ing the sense and value of their baptism. The method is to form
communities of NCs within parishes, sadly quite separate, especially in worship, from the rest of the parish.

It goes without saying that there is a deep crisis of faith within
contemporary society and a great disillusionment with things
spiritual in general and with the church and religion in particular. I believe this is not so much a deliberate conscious opposi-
tion, but an apathy and disappointment that is deep seated. The
materialism and individualism which is at the heart of contemporary life is seen to make the church irrelevant. Even the traditional celebration of rites of passage such as baptism, marriage
and even death, along with the major Christian celebrations like
Easter and Christmas, are in decline. There is I believe a basic
feeling of lovelessness, even loneliness and desolation. The
church does not seem, in spite of so many efforts at renewal, to
address this contemporary situation in an effective way. So
many people struggle for meaning and dignity and for clues to
the human puzzle. This century, with its history of human suffering on a scale hardly ever imagined before, produces atheism;
especially when the church with its powerful gift of the Holy
Spirit to unburden people, to lift burdens from people's backs,
often is so bound and burdened itself, that it cannot fulfil its
God-given ministry to the world. Even when presented with the
contemporary awful suffering of AIDS, the church still, I believe,
stubbornly holds onto outmoded ways of sexual health, which if
changed would at least ease the spread of this catastrophic illness. I'm not for one moment saying that the church has nothing
to offer – that would be ludicrous – but I believe what has been
said in recent times in this area by senior churchmen is not helpful for poor suffering humanity.

So in this context there can be something very attractive in a movement which says we are the 'Way', we can find you the answers.

Restlessness begets meaninglessness, and the lack of meaning in life is a soul sadness, whose full extent and full import our age has not yet begun to comprehend.

(C. C. Jung, *The Structures and the Dynamics of the Psyche*)

So it's either total disintegration or effective renewal. It is a fact that many parishes cannot rise to such a challenge and, with a cocktail of poor liturgy, poor preaching, and poor music, the scene is set for the inevitable tragedy of empty churches. Even in the diocese of Rome there is a sad picture of parish life which mirrors parishes and dioceses throughout the western world.

'There is a weariness and a tiredness. The fact that some people come to believe that a pseudo-religious sect ... has more to offer than a mainline church reflects on all our churches and we should be ashamed and challenged by it.' *(Dr Thomas Butler, Bishop of Leicester)*

The fact that such fundamentalism comes about is of no surprise. The fact that a group like the NCs should spring up at this time is almost to be expected. It's a movement of desperation and I must say part of me has a sympathy for it. Again the Bishop of Leicester writes:

'Some people succumb, if they have been pushed hard enough with certainty, when they feel vulnerable under the pressures of life. Some are moved by the prospect of instant family, when their own lives are poor in friendship. Some are tempted by a message which seems to give a meaningto existence when their lives are confused.'

There is an enormous amount of uncertainty in life and the fundamentalist tries to escape this dreadful insecurity by clinging on for grim death to a certainty which does not in fact exist. The Christian journey is about transcendent security and the challenge to trust. 'I am disturbed by those who have terrible doubts about religion, but I am even more disturbed by those who have terrible certainties!' *(Dr Thomas Butler, Bishop of Leicester)*

'Fundamentalism is another pseudo mysticism, whether it comes from the Protestant literalism of the Bible and the television evangelists' Word of God message, from the literalism of Roman Catholics looking for salvation by way of papal announcements, or Muslims hanging on to the word of the Ayatollah ... Because these fundamentalist movements always lack the integrity of justice, deep violence lurks just beneath their sentimentalisms. Sadly they have the power to seduce into their narrowly sectarian ways the young who are searching for true community and vision ...'

Jacobi and Hill, 'The Rise of Cults is a Lack of Mysticism in Today's Religious Institutions'.

I was almost seduced into joining the NC. I liked their liturgy which was prayerful and creative and the families who were already members when I came onto the scene were lovely. I had just left the priestly therapeutic centre so I was an ideal candidate.

What I found interesting was the feeling of the rest of the parish – the majority in fact. It was a sort of *sensus fidelium* that touched me – that feeling in the people of God for what is good and what isn't. Many felt that they were second-class citizens and were deemed not worth spending time with. Because the NC community celebrated a separate Sunday liturgy they never really met up with the rest of the parish. They even had their own Easter Vigil. The only answer the parish priest had to people who came to him with their problems was to join the NC movement. Too many wavering reeds were being crushed, too many flickering flames snuffed out.

People in the NC movement were being encouraged to marry within the movement. The very first NC marriage sadly fell apart and they came to me to help them start the annulment process, which was eventually granted. People who left the NC movement were abandoned, but a nember of courageous, inspired parishioners set up a group that both welcomed people back to the parish, helped to de-brief them, and petitioned the bishop to initiate an investigation. We were greatly helped and supported by one of the Vicars General of the diocese.

I was told by one of the children in the NC that I had been declared an enemy of the 'Way' and there should be no connection with me. Many left the parish, one family found the local Church of England church a better option. I felt very lonely indeed. Thank God for the support of the parish. Eventually after seven years the bishop forbade them, after a long and detailed enquiry, to exist in the diocese.

I mention all of the above to emphasise both the immense difficulty and challenge to us all to renew our inner selves and the church and society at large, to explore the complex nature of this process in the contemporary world. The intentions behind the Neo-Catechumenate movement I believe are good ones, but the price to be paid for its methods is too high at the level of human freedom and dignity. It produces, from my experience, a sin-sodden mentality, where the unbinding of our humanity, a gift given to the church especially, and the lifting of burdens from each others backs, is somewhat neglected. I do not deny that some people have grown as persons and have had a new spiritual awakening through this movement and others like it, just as some Catholics do from saying the rosary every day and reciting almost disappeared litanies and devotions.

But the more I listen to my own heart and soul, the more I hear what people are saying around me today. I feel we need to be exploring and experiencing different ways to the soul and to this often elusive God of ours. Of all the poems of R. S. Thomas, quoted in this book, the one I'm going to quote now I feel is the most disturbing, though I am at the level of not fully yet being able to grasp it:

And God said, 'I will build a Church here
And cause this people to worship me,
And afflict them with poverty and sickness
In return for centuries of hard work
And patience. And its windows let in the light
Grudgingly, as their minds do, and the priests words will be
    drowned
By the wind's caterwauling,

... All this I will do, said God, and watch the bitterness in
   their eyes
Grow, and their lips supperate with
Their prayers. And their women shall bring forth
On my altars, and I will choose the best
Of them to be thrown back into the sea.
And that was only on one island!
(R. S. Thomas, *The Island*)

Recently our organisation T.H.O.M.A.S. won the Pride of
Lancashire award. As well as winning the top vote in our cate-
gory, we won the overall vote of the readers of the *Lancashire
Evening Telegraph*. Now I know that this is not exactly world
shattering, but I have a point to make here. At the moment our
church, which was arsoned, is now almost rebuilt and ready for
the bishop to come and re-consecrate. A few of the people who
have put their energy into the rebuilding of the church (half the
original size now) love what it stands for. The main spiritual
events of their lives have taken place within these walls. But on
the Sunday morning after the presentation of the Pride of
Lancashire awards to T.H.O.M.A.S. there was criticism from
these basically good people about the work we are doing with
the homeless and addicted, the lost and the pained. To me both
are connected deeply. We need buildings that are dedicated to
God's glory, sacred empty spaces which symbolise how much
there is to be filled in our own personal lives; but equally
important – well maybe not equally important, but rather more
important – is to rebuild the living temples of God's presence in
those on the edge of life.

   As R. S. Thomas reflects in the poem above, we can build our
churches till the cows come home and be unaware of our sickness of soul and our inner poverty which can make our hearts so
hard, no matter how long we spend within the sacred walls.
There can be little light penetrating through into our minds to
enlarge them, and we become concerned with the trappings of
religion and the fripperies of faith. R. S. Thomas indicated that
our moving lips that utter our well-worn prayers could be lips

filled with putrefaction. They are no longer lips that will willingly kiss the leper and lead us to hold the untouchable. But the temple presence of God and the very hands-on work with those in need, to me are inseparable for the believer.

What connects all of these things is the eucharist. The bread of the eucharist is always broken if it is to be shared. The blood of Christ poured out for all. The eucharist changes us, our thinking, our looking, our touching.

One of the early descriptions of the eucharist is the story in Luke's gospel of the two disciples on the road to Emmaus. They walk along together, these two friends who had known Jesus, and now thought he was dead and gone. We are told that they walked together, away from the holy city and the temple heavily downcast. Being downcast can also mean being cast down by the life experiences that come our way. It's not unknown to do a 'geographical' when reality feels too tough to deal with, and take our pain to another place, but not to another dimension.

The Emmaus story proceeds with the unrecognised Christ joining these two. It's amazing how popular the poem 'Footsteps' is. It's a bit sentimental, but does contain a dash of scriptural theology – that experience of being carried, or accompanied by something, someone, when we can't walk anymore on our own or pray or feel.

In the story Christ engages these two downcast people in a question and answer conversation. At the eucharist, of course, we bring ourselves as we are at that moment before the love and mercy and kindness of God as he speaks to us in the scriptures. What is important for us, like for the two on the road to Emmaus, is how we respond to that word there and then. Does it touch our souls, our hearts and minds at the moment of impact?

We are told in the Emmaus story that when the conversation had ended, Christ made as if to go on. But they insisted that he stay. This is our challenge too. 'Stay with us, for it is nearly evening, the day is almost over.' (Luke 24:29) Sometimes we don't utter these words until our lives are almost over and the

dark veil of faith is all we have to cling to. But we can invite him
to stay, long before this. If we do he will break the bread of life
with us and give new hope, new vision, and new possibilities.
He will give us courage to look at ourselves and maybe return to
that which we have been running away from for so long, and to
some he will give the grace to be ambassadors to his resurrection, to his eucharistic presence, and to the connection between
all of this with people fractured and damaged by life.

> … On a bare
> Hill a bare tree saddened
> The sky. Many people
> Held out their thin arms
> To it, as though waiting
> For a vanished April
> To return to it's crossed
> Boughs. The son watched
> Them. Let me go there, he said.
> (R. S. Thomas, *The Coming*)

Those 'thin arms' mean so much to me today. As a run up to
World AIDS Day the media has been presenting some very good
and disturbing documentaries. The universal pain and suffering
connected with AIDS is of gargantuan proportions. I have a
deep ache inside which I expressed in a sermon I gave in
Blackburn Cathedral this World AIDS Day. There is no doubt in
my mind that in certain areas of social health for those who are
HIV positive, we as a church have got part of our pastoral approach wrong. We are working I believe from bad intelligence in
this area. Not completely, because the church is at work in many
branches of care related to HIV and AIDS. I have thought and
prayed hard about this and I've worked alongside many gay
people and people with HIV and AIDS and I feel that some
Catholics, even senior churchmen, have been prevented from
showing genuine effective love and service to those who do not
conform in the expression of their sex lives to Catholic teaching.
The ministry of its prophetic role in the world has been affected
– unobtainable high standards of behaviour for the 'thin armed

poor' of this world is a contemporary scandal – they are waiting for that 'vanished April' and I believe longing for the church to say 'let me go there'.

The 'prayed out' experience of this book has led me into the place where the poor, or those on the edge, as I prefer to call us, are. I've never felt more right at being where I am. Not necessarily comfortable, but right. One of the attributes of the people of no importance is that they always have to wait for things. Nothing comes early or quickly. This has given me time to wait before God in a sort of attentive prayed-outness. I am a person who definitely needs the order of public liturgy in my life. When I do sit alone with the alone it's always a different experience each time, but with the underlying theme of feeling incomplete. I've always been looking for that missing bit in my life but, as I've indicated above, never really found it in a person or place or thing.

Waiting on God has taught me a little more about detachment. I feel I no longer cling nor want to, to friends, even my closest. I feel that my priesthood is not mine. It was given to me by God through the church thirty years ago, and the expression of it has changed so much since that cold February day in 1974. This detachment does not mean I don't feel deeply or passionately, in fact it seems to heighten my feelings. I'm beginning to see that I am so small in all of this cosmic process. I am beginning to thank God, distant though he often seems through the dark veil of faith, for just being part of things, no matter how small.

A few years ago a colleague of mine called Dorothy, who has gone on to found a very special, contemplative, yet action-filled ministry to those on the edge, in a neighbouring town, helped a friend and myself present an Advent retreat day. The title of it was 'A Small Nondescript Place' – it was a meditation on Advent and the birth of Christ.

Dorothy Ann McGregor, who is I believe a contemporary mystic, had the bottom line approach to all, especially the little one's of this world, to make a heaven of the margins a sort of icon which is a window into the divine – nothing sentimental, but with the discipline of prayer and radical dedication. To give you an indication of contemporary attentiveness to God in our world I'm going to comment on some of the spirituality of that day and basically of Dorothy Ann McGregor.

Dorothy to some extent looks at the world as I do – though she is far more advanced on the road to spiritual maturity than I am. When I look at the Manger, for example, I already see the imprint of the passion … This was to be a new way of life:

No-one would be excluded,
no-one rejected. And all the
wasted splintered broken-down people
who suffer in dire despair … would
be counted and embraced in an infinite
regarding! *(Dorothy Ann McGregor)*

Christ who was born in a nondescript place can also be born over and over again in the hidden lives of people. Our lives can touch many if we try to live one day at a time, not by being pious, but by being in touch with our brokenness, our frailty, our fears, our anger and our doubts. His birth was a choice, 'send me'. Christ showed us alongside his death, a way to celebrate life, as a festival, a journey not really meaningless even though for me it has often felt that way, but something to be grasped hold of.

When this Christ is born in us we no longer need to squander our lives in self-destructive behaviour. Attentiveness, prayer is the key to bring together heaven and earth. When we do pray no matter how poorly, we begin to glimpse the world as God sees it – we want to bless rather than curse, inspire rather than denigrate, be alongside others, counting them as special.

The journey from the stable to Calvary is one journey. The light of the star leading wise men gives way to a darkness which covered the earth on that terribly awesome day 'we ache for the illusion of love'. *(Dorothy Ann McGregor)*

I guess that is why so many find Christmas disappointing – we have an illusion about family, and being together, we forget how imperfect and frail we really are. 'The message of Christmas is that goodness will shine wherever it exists, perhaps, not conquering evil, but as a prerequisite for facing it … Every time we approach Christmas we have another opportunity to bring a song to the lips of our souls.' *(Dorothy Ann McGregor)*

This is just a taste of Dorothy Ann McGregor's spirituality, which is mine also. I like this approach – it's fresh, it's honest, it feels right.

The journey to prayed-out, to attentiveness to God in all things, is a harsh yet exciting journey. I've had to let go of so much, with the emptiness of not knowing for certain. I'm not sure of so much, I'm not sure who I am or who I'm meant to be. I'm not sure where God is taking me. My reality is a mystery, but at the same time it feels real. As Gregory of Nyssa commented on Abraham's faith to follow where God wanted him to be: 'It was only when Abraham did not know where he was going that he learned he was going the right way.'

I'm trying to work on not having too many regrets for what I might have been, but this is difficult for me. But one thing I am learning, thanks to the spirituality of people like Dorothy Ann McGregor, is that no one is too small or too insignificant to love. No life is futile, no matter how short.

The Mass of Christ which I am privileged to celebrate, is the Mass of those on the edges – who keep bringing me back to stark reality and keep reminding me that it's never too late nor the task too impossible and that

'… one life is enough.' *(Dorothy Ann McGregor)*

CHAPTER NINE

Late in Love's school

'My ears had heard of you, but now my eyes have seen you.'
(Job 42:5)

We met
under a shower
of bird notes.
fifty years passed
love's moment
in a world in
servitude to time
she was young;
I kissed with my eyes
Closed and opened
Then on her wrinkles.
'Come!' Said death,
choosing her as his
partner for
the last dance. And she,
who in life
had done everything
with a bird's grace,
opened her bill now
for the shedding
of one sigh no
heavier than a feather.
(R. S. Thomas, *A Marriage*)

In the poem above R. S. Thomas reflects on his life-long love for his wife and, even with his own personal theological questioning and his wrestling with the things of God and even God himself, he lets his wife depart with grace and dignity and with the romantic image of a 'last dance'.

For me after over fifty years of living, of loving another human being, albeit imperfectly, as well as trying to love God, I have been changed repeatedly and often imperceptibly. For me though, love, real love, has come late – and my whole being is stirred when I see love so tender and grace-filled in the young and in those couples whose love has stood the test of time, and is even deeper, if that is possible, when the loved one is danced away in death.

St Paul, reflecting on his conversion experience and his mid-life call to a new direction and ministry, calls himself 'the least of the apostles'. (Ephesians 2:8) He also writes of himself like this '... and last of all he appeared to me also as to one born unexpected'. (Corinthians 15:8)

After a hedonistic and pagan background and one illegitimate daughter, St Augustine writes in his *Confessions*,

'Late as I loved you beauty so ancient and so new. I looked for you outside of myself, but all the while you were within.'

It goes beyond one's imaginings today that men like Paul of Tarsus and Augustine, with all their antecedent behaviour, could possibly be considered by the church for the office of bishop. Maybe we don't really believe these days in conversion of life, that complete turn around that only God can orchestrate. It's a pity really. I guess there could be some very effective bishops out there who have undergone this process; who could bring the transforming power of God's grace to such a ministry and touch the minds and souls of so many. We run scared today as a church, like the rest of official life. We must be seen to be politically correct, even to the extremes of France, where no religious or spiritual symbols can be seen in public schools. It's hard to imagine that France, once called by historians 'the eldest daughter of the church', should ban even the cross from public view. I hope the iconoclasts will not be let loose on the beautiful religious buildings of their country.

Being late, or even feeling lost in the school of love, is something fascinating for me. In my daily practical life I'm usually on time or even early for things. But a lot of the things I am on time for, are sometimes not that important, and in the past I've been very late and even not there at all for the more important things.

For me entering into this last quarter of my life, if it takes the natural course, is both exciting and challenging, and frightening. In my more reflective moments I realise so profoundly how small I am in this short stay here. This came home to me just before Christmas when I was out walking with a young friend of mine, whose marriage I celebrated a year or two ago and which has now fallen apart. We had been walking together on the top of Pendle Hill in Lancashire on that winter afternoon. There was a piercing cold with a clear blue sky. We saw at the same time a large winter sun setting over Kemple End and at the opposite end of Pendle Hill, a full moon rising from behind it – it was awesome. Almost immediately after seeing, this we noticed something red in the heather. When we walked over to it, we discovered a Christmas wreath with newly scattered ashes. It again came home even more to me the smallness of my being – there in the background the sun and the moon with millions of years of life in them, my young friend pouring out his sadness and me with my lifesworth and here, the symbol of the end of all our journeys searching, a handful of ashes, on a moor in Lancashire – with the world below getting on with it as it always does.

The idea of arriving late, to that which is of supreme importance, is a strange one. For me, I thought I'd arrived at where I was meant to be when I was ordained a priest at 25 years of age. I thought then that the gift of priesthood was the greatest that God would ever give me. Great as it is, God had some other gifts in the wings that would be greater. The gift of being able to love and receive love and eventually to have a deep friendship with another human being; to experience a conversion, not dramatic but often ponderously even boringly slow, being saved by grace alone from the abyss and the dragon I pass daily, apparently sleeping, but not really and with a ferocious appetite; the gift also of being 'prayed out' and then being shown how prayer alone would save me from this devouring beast, always crouching at my door.

At one level it's been a journey back to the beginning. Looking at it dispassionately, my life has had a very clear beginning, a middle that was even more complex, and an ending which brought me back to the whole faith and prayer experience, though very much changed by the dynamics of it all. And of course even though it feels like a beginning, a middle and an end, the end is not really the end. The section of my life that I'm in now feels like a new story with its own beginning and middle and I guess the end being death itself.

I've used the image of dance and ballet in the chapter 'Unfaithful', because dance has something of beauty and grace about it. It's what lovers do, it's what in a way comes naturally to most people. In dancing we forget our environment and just let our bodies and spirits play.

'… begin the music, shake the tambourine.' (Ps 81:2)

And to dance with God is wilder and more exciting than is possible to imagine.

'I will take hold of your hand …' (Isaiah 41:6)

About seeing the familiar, or our starting point, properly, T. S. Eliot reminds us that after all our journeying we end up where we started from recognising it for the first time.

I'm just beginning to understand what this is all about. I used to try and forget some of my particular beginnings, quite simply because they were not always that pleasant. I feel I unsuccessfully tried to re-invent myself and present myself to the world wearing whatever mask I thought appropriate for the occasion. I had a large collection of masks. It's interesting for me that my experience of human love and lust and sin all mixed up together should have taken place in the city of many masks – Venice. Venice of course, and all that started there as written in the chapter 'Unfaithful', was again one of those many beginnings of something that I wanted at one level to forget or at least keep away from the public gaze. But not any more. St Augustine wrote his *Confessions*, and I feel this process helped him to accept the realities of his past so that his present had more strength to it. To know that such a spiritual giant as Thomas Merton the American Cistercian monk, also sired a child in his younger years, is not so much something to be scandalised by, but a sign of the power of grace which brought him to a conversion of life.

We know that God's grace is present in the seven sacraments for sure, but his grace is not confined to the seven sacraments. It is an incredible extravagant free gift of God. It makes saints out of sinners. Peter, who denied even knowing Christ, became the rock of faith. The disciples who all left him eventually gave their lives for him. Paul who put Christians to death became the great apostle to the Gentiles. Augustine, a man of the world with a very active sex life, became a bishop, theologian and saint and is still influencing the church today. Ignatius of Loyola, who after being injured out of the army, thought about taking his own life, established the Jesuit congregation that has had a massive influence on the church from the Counter Reformation, to the missions in China, right down to the present day.

And closer to home, a woman called Dorothy Ann McGregor, whom I have quoted from in the chapter 'Attentiveness the Heart of Prayer – Out or In', in a recent interview for the *Guardian*, spoke of her denial of God for the first half of her life and of recovery from mental breakdown. Now she lives a contemplative life in the middle of Accrington, Lancashire, and runs a centre for the ones who find themselves on the edge of everything. She fasts and prays, and like the prophetess Hannah – she rarely leaves the temple of God's presence.

I bring myself to this list which could go on and on – not in the sense of being some spiritual giant – that I'm not – but as someone who has been led I believe by the grace of God alone into another way of living, albeit imperfect and with much stumbling. My human nature with my character defects is still alive and active. The only real safeguard for me is the constancy of prayer, even when it is arid. Also the development of good friendships, where I can try to be unselfish and where I can be a person who has something life-enhancing to offer.

I'm also aware that there is always the danger of self-deception in all of this. Am I, by writing this, trying to convince myself of the truth of it all? I have to keep asking myself honest questions like, if I'd met Dom today would my decision be different? I have to ask do I stay within my Order and in the priesthood, because I can't really do anything else? How do I know what is true and genuine? The poet Louis MacNeice writes

And if the world were black and white entirely
And all the charts were plain
Instead of a mad weir of tigerish waters,
A prism of delight and pain,
We might be surer where we wished to go
… but in brute reality there is no
Road that is right entirely.
(Louis MacNeice, *Entirely*)

I think deep down my longing, like C. S. Lewis's, is not so much for a place like heaven, but for a person. And there is a sort of internal conflict that goes on. Is the person I desire God, or is the person I am looking for another human being? If I found the right person to love as I thought I had once, would that be the same as finding God? Certainly my training and spirituality of the distant past emphasised that God was enough, and that I didn't need close and intimate relationships. But the result of being faithful to all of this for me was unspeakable loneliness and troubled thoughts. As the years have gone by, and I look back at how I handled all of these issues, I know for certain that I handled them badly. I produced for myself a sort of dichotomy, with God on one side and my needy humanity on the other. The two never met and this polarisation of experiences produced a sort of emotional disintegration. Now I can put into words what I really want and try to synthesise the God thing and the human love thing.

John Donne speaks of the old Adam in Genesis and the New Adam, Christ, meeting in him. He also writes in one of his 'Holy Sonnets':

Batter my heart, three-person'd God …
I, like a usurped towne, to another due,

> Labour to admit you, but oh to no end …
> … Take me to you, imprison mee, for I
> Except you enthral mee, never shall be free,
> Nor ever chaste, except you ravish me.
> (John Donne, *Batter my Heart*)

This strong, emotional and metaphysical poetry of course reveals the internal battle that rages in the human heart. People will always ask, 'Where is God?' 'What is love? 'Is this the right decision for me?'

It seems to me that part of the process of entering into a deep relationship of love with another person, or with God, is not to focus on myself but on the other, and with God the one who is totally 'Other' than I am.

I have discovered little by little the presence of the totally 'Other' in the events of each day. Each moment is a gift and it's not a dress rehearsal for anything. The extravagance of God's love is beyond my intellect, but the signs of it are there for me to discover and feel. The Incarnation speaks to me of the extravagant love of God. Duns Scotus, the medieval Franciscan theologian, wrote that even if humanity had not sinned and had not needed the Redemption, Christ would have still been born and lived with us out of unspeakable and extravagant love, because that is God's nature. But the reality is even more wonderful in that he showed us that profound love, when we did turn away from him. He is for all of us forever.

This for me is demonstrated with that other extravagant gift from Christ, the eucharist, and of course forever linked with this, the washing of the feet. For a long time as the previous chapters hint, I carried round with me like a child carries round a favourite cuddly toy as a comforter, the brokenness of my constant weary beginnings, the loneliness of endings, the deception of me to myself and the despair of myself. And because this had gone on for so long I thought that I was going to be too late to reconnect with this God of mine. Even so, through love, mostly prayer and some therapy, I moved on and others have helped to cut the ropes holding all these burdens in my soul and heart and mind. Except for one, which for some hidden psycho-spiritual reason, I don't want to let go of. Dom I could never let go of and carry on with the ease of contemporary popular psychology, pretending that it doesn't hurt, or that some sense could be made of it. I know the theology, I know that Christ has entered the world, my world; that he has tasted rejection, carried each person's sense of failure, shared each betrayed person's anguish, penetrated each experience of forsakenness and tasted death for us all. I know all of this and the immediacy of forgiveness.

God has been gracious to me; at one level I'm graced to be still alive. I don't believe in luck, or in fate, but I do believe in a divine plan. Even though I cannot always make sense of my everydays and even though on some days I despair of myself, I know from faith alone, which of course is God's grace, that there is a deep down purpose in every moment of every day. Like God, just because I don't experience it, or acknowledge it, doesn't mean it's not there.

I've often complained that for a long time now I wake up very early. I'm usually out of bed by half-past five in the morning. But I gradually discovered what a gift this is. Apart from some good Italian coffee from the luxury of my coffee-making machine – I am quite comfortably drawn to what once felt burdensome – I say the morning prayer of the church, and then celebrate the eucharist. I write at this time; I clean and iron at this time and three mornings a week I go to the gym.

This newly discovered love for me has its foundation in the eucharist. More and more I feel drawn into this sacred mystery where my real life is revealed to me and I am united with the whole church, especially those on the edge. And I find as I look back over the years that, as well as a proclivity to sadness and brokenness, I've always been near the edge in my ministry. Young people I worked with ask me to come to their weddings and baptise their children; sometimes to help them with annulments and on one occasion to conduct the funeral of someone who died from AIDS. Working on a help-line for confused and often pained people, who struggle with being gay or lesbian and who are trying to make sense of it all. Saying Mass for Catholic gay people, who feel often the painful dichotomy of trying to live a Christian life with largely unhelpful words from the Congregation for the Doctrine of the Faith. The list goes on and on and the daily reminder in my work with the homeless, and those on our residential re-hab, of just how close it all is, to capitulate and give up – and then I see people who have not had my choices and privileges, grow and mature and get clean and well. All this to me these days is about God's love for us. It's not all about the pain in people's lives either. There are more glimpses of happiness these days and as G. M. Hopkins writes about God'

    … and dost thou touch me afresh?

    Over again I feel thy finger and find thee.

    (G. M. Hopkins, *The Wreck of the Deutschland*)

To be touched afresh by God is truly amazing. There is an excitement contained in this quotation. It can be great to let go of the parental hand, but sometimes to lose contact with that hand for too long can have its own desperate consequences. But finding the finger over and over again is of course about God's profound love and fathomless mercy. There is an old hymn I remember vaguely from my youth. I think it's called, 'Jesu the very thought of Thee'. A line from the hymn says:

    Ah but to those who find

    Ah this, none but his lovers know.

I was surprised when the controversial Bishop Jenkins once bishop of Durham, whose theology, especially about the Resurrection shocked quite a lot of people, cited this on a programme as one of his favourite hymns.

    The way God's love comes into all our different lives has a deep mystery and variety around it. Often in the middle of what in my life has appeared to be, and felt like being, abandoned to emptiness – let loose like a toddler in a shopping precinct to the spirals of unending space – comes the discovery of the 'Other', and that I have never really been alone. I've known for years that there has always been a better way than the 'via negativa'. I've always known deep down that there was another way through, besides the psychiatrist's couch or the doctor's surgery, or the sleepless nights, or the fears, the loneliness and the deadness inside.

God has shown me profound love in his presence in others. When a young guy showed me the marks where he had once slashed his wrists, it was an icon of Christ in the upper room – the fear-ridden and weak disciples locked in after the crucifixion are shown the marks of the nails and the spear in Christ's now risen body. It was a symbol of contemporary life and a mirror image of mine. Just because my pain was not quite so visible except to the really perceptive, who could go beyond the very often shallow, happy exterior, it was no less real.

I also realise today that the only reason that I am still on my journey at all is because of my brothers and sisters who walk with me. It's basically about the power of the ministry of one person to another. It's the celebration of the mystery of faith; it's a statement about the reality of Jesus Christ.

For so many years, like Augustine I looked for fulfilment, love, meaning outside of myself. I had not really the courage to make that journey to the centre of myself. I know intellectually that my deep yearnings were yearnings for God. But I never really felt that he was at the centre of my being. But through grace I was driven on by a hunger and a thirst that could never be satisfied outside of God.

Just in case you think some miraculous event has taken place in my conversion, I would like to add that it's not over till its over. The party's not over till the fat lady sings, even though I have come late to discover the difference between lust and love, and have a dash more gratitude for the divinity touching my humanity. I can still only play the piano of my life with one finger. Even though it's the road to God that matters these days, it is still a mysterious road with lots of blind bends and people who stop me and ground me and help save me.

… and inbetween one the false starts, the failures,

the ruins from which we climbed …

God it is not your reflections

we seek, wonderful as they are
in the live fibre; it is the possibility
of your presence at the core's
point towards which we soar
in hope to arrive at the still
centre, where love operates
on all those frequencies
that are set up by the spinning
of two minds, the one of the other.'
(R. S. Thomas, *Cones*)

Yes, 'now my eyes have seen you.' (Job 42:5)

CHAPTER TEN

A Nondescript Place

'When you were younger you dressed yourself and went where you
wanted; but when you are old you will stretch out your hand and
someone else will dress and lead you where you do not want to go.'
(John: 21:18)

One of the first things I realised as a student for the priesthood,
in the context of a religious community where we daily said the
office together, was the apparent contradiction of things. At one
moment a psalm would be speaking about the hiddenness of the
God of Israel, and another suggesting that none of us could escape his presence. Even in the depth of the underworld, he was
there. He was the one who knew us before we were born and
had carved our names on the palm of his hand.

His promises, like his absence and presence, seemed to contra-
dict as well. Even if our father and mother should forsake us, he
would never abandon us, because he loves us with an everlasting
love. Yet we could be told to depart from him into the everlasting
darkness that had been prepared for the devil and his angels.

These revealed truths of scripture, with their apparent contradictions, are also reflected in my experience of myself and
others. My ideals for myself, my hopes for myself, are often
thwarted by the reality of my experiences. At one moment my
passionate heart and soul longs for the beauty and harmony of
things. It longs for love and then it can turn to that which is so
self-centred and empty, filled with self-destructive thoughts
and sometimes behaviour.

I've asked myself over the years, since I entered religious life
aged eighteen, was it for all of this that I gave my promise to
him? The simple answer is 'yes'. Anyone who is called to be a
lover comes to the place of what I call painful waiting. On reflec-
tion, the meaning of something deeper is in the waiting – if we

stop waiting, we stop loving. There is a sense in the nonsense, there is knowing in not knowing, there is finding by losing, there is hope by hoping against hope. We trail into our lives the darkness and the light together.

All through scripture, from Genesis to the Apocalypse, this reality of contraries meeting in the same person is as much part of the human condition as is existential loneliness. Even in this there is contradiction. God is at the centre of our very lives and existence, the world is crowded with his images and often we connect in deep love with another human being, and yet there is loneliness – a sadness that goes hand in hand with our freedom. Often I've experienced my mind fractured by my life experiences and my soul scarred.

I feel there is in modern psychology a great untruth, a deception which is very easy to be sucked into. In the Book of Genesis the serpent convinces Adam that he can be master of his own destiny and that he does not need to depend on God – he can handle his life. So many psychology books I believe peddle this untruth and lead so many, myself included in the past, to live out the drama of life like a cheap soap opera, going no deeper than the surface of things. Playing at being a human being, acting and acting out our fantasies of what life and love is all about.

William Blake wrote about this destructive temptation to attachment to things that of their very nature are passing and fleeting:

… rather than binding ourselves to joy,
we must kiss it, as it flies.
(William Blake, *Eternity*)

All of us, I believe, if we could only give it the time it deserves, would come to the conclusion that we are eternal, to reflect on Spinoza's thoughts. But I like so many others had to undergo God's loving surgery, where he kept removing things and people from me, in order that they may be saved as well as me. Being exiled from my false idea of a Garden of Eden, and exiled from my false ideas of self, were not so much a punishment, though painful, but a redeeming process for me.

I can become so easily addicted to the imprisoning slavery of living my life on the surface of things, never having the courage to go deep. Any sort of addiction is at war with freedom, and freedom is the gift from God. But there are so many pitfalls on the road to recovery, whether it be from substance misuse or that addiction which is an attachment to self and usually contains such a powerful ego that we have managed to create, which turns into something like Frankenstein's monster and is out to destroy us.

I've learned a lot from the young people on our residential rehab at T.H.O.M.A.S. – both those who have managed good, clean time and sobriety and those who still struggle. One of the main things I've learned is how cunning and seductive the thinking around this is. For example, the actual physical removal from where addicts fed and lived out their addiction, can at one level be like entering a fantasy world where one feels freed from the addiction's need to be constantly obeyed – but after leaving this environment the reality can be shocking. Even after so long in such withdrawal from the old environment, when entering it again, starting back to the old behaviour of using is not uncommon.

My spiritual journey, any spiritual journey is similar. There isn't and never has been, I believe, a sort of Golden Period for the church or spirituality – it is always about the struggle for what is real in a very tough and lonely environment we call the universe. As in the recovery process from addiction to mind altering chemicals, so on my road to God I must be aware of the tricks my mind can play on me. I've thought so many times that I've had a real conversion experience – but it was only when the purgation process became real for me, a complete breakdown and exhaustion of what I thought was the real me, when I stopped wearing all the masks, that I began to get a glimpse that maybe the pain and the struggles, the hopelessness and the almost despair were somehow blessed. This was to offer me at least a fighting chance to transcend my idols and take the risk of going deep into the one and only chance I had, in my three score

years and ten, to allow the only life I would ever have, to be
saved, not by myself – that's the illusion – but by the grace of
God at work in my very being, a being that would disintegrate
into emptiness and nothingness, if my God did not constantly
keep me in his heart.

The title of this last chapter 'A Nondescript Place' is about
what seems to me to be a whole pattern of things in my life. It's
about coming to the conclusion, late in the day, that my life and
all the people and experiences I've had and hopefully will still
have, are to be discovered in the poverty and littleness of self.
Everything is on loan, or leased out to me. All the people I care
for, the few I've actually dared to try to love, my priesthood, my
every breath is something that ultimately belongs to another.

> a life's trivia: commit them
> not to the page, but to the waste-basket
> of time. What was special
> about you? …
> … You ran fast and came home breathless.
>
> Among scanty possessions fear
> was yours. Courage you borrowed
> on short loan;
>
> And one came to your back door
> all bones and in rags, asking the kiss
> that would have transformed both you
> and him; and you would not,
> slamming it in his face. Only
> to find him waiting at your bed's side.
> (R. S. Thomas, *Biography*)

At one level I feel that some of my dreams and nightmares have
shown me things that I feel are part of the redemptive process
offered by God. Like Scrooge after his visitations by the three
ghostly spectres – the past, the present and the most fearful of
all, the future, I wake up to find that it is still Christmas morning
and that deep down call to conversion, change, is still possible. I
must say though time sometimes feels to be rushing by, years

seem to end more suddenly. Often my thoughts do go to the winter of the grave and wonder how it will be.

I am always aware of the magnitude of the shadows in my life, especially when they have involved others whom I have hurt, or damaged by my self will. It's always been difficult for me to try and work out the purposes of the one who is eternal. I would give anything I have that is good in my life, to redress what happened to Dom – and I do mean anything. But my history is my history and in a rather chilling verse from R. S. Thomas, there is the stark reality of what this means.

But time passes by;
it commits adultery
with it to father its cause
of its continual weeping.
(R. S. Thomas, *History*)

And yet all of this I must bring to this God of mine, otherwise despair is the only consequence.

The mysterious visitor in the poem 'Biography' quoted above, who comes to the back door only to be pushed away and then is seen again '… waiting at your bedside' – who is this visitor – is it the grim reaper? Would embracing the reality of my mortality earlier in life, have prevented the consequences of pride ruling my will and made me more humble and more in touch with reality?

But the great thing is that God gives us so many opportunities of responding to his ever present love. To be able to come through, or be carried through the Gethsemane of things which make what was once seemingly impossible, possible, is part of the gist of what it means to be a sharer in what resurrection means. It's the end of promoting the phoney self and the shallow living out of half a life – it's about a new sort of space to grow in. For so long being alive for me meant nothing. There was that death of ideals and hopes, but a necessary one. I thought once I had loved someone possibly, and maybe that is true, but now it's about loving unconditionally.

The love that flows through us as we empty ourselves of ourselves makes us lovable and precious, just as it makes others so. It is up to each of us whether we reflect light or darkness, goodness or negativity. It doesn't matter whether our place in life is greater or smaller. When there is no separation between time and timelessness, space and spacelessness, finiteness and eternity, we become co-creators with the One, and become our true selves.

(Dorothy Anne McGregor, *And Love Dwells There*)

To come to our true selves and not be too afraid eventually at what we find and see is a great privilege and is nothing less than gift. The truth, as Jesus taught in the gospel, will set us free, no matter how awful the truth might be. To be free is to say one lived a life filled with hope and opportunity and also responsibility.

'I must keep alive – myself ... press on to that other country and ... help others to do the same.'

(C. S. Lewis, *Mere Christianity*)

I'm writing this final chapter one year on from when I started this book and Lent looms large, beginning next Wednesday. I've been asked by the Dean of Blackburn's Anglican Cathedral to lead the Stations of the Cross there during Holy Week. This traditional Lenten prayer seems to me to be about waiting around for something. Like standing on railway stations for arrivals and departures and cancellations.

The hill of Calvary, for which the infant of Christmas night was born and waited, is not so much a hill to preach from, but rather one to stumble and ascend towards. The whole of Christ's life was about waiting for this 'hour'.

The passion for me begins in Bethlehem in the house of bread and starts to dramatically unfold in the upper room where the eucharist is instituted at the Passover meal. Here, there is a letting go of things and people and promises. From this room Judas leaves to betray Christ and the dark night begins. Peter promises the earth and is diminished by his shrill and hollow words. In Gethsemane Christ waits for God to speak to him, but

gets nothing only sweat and tears and the noise of snoring disciples. He then waits for the tree of the cross to loom up in darkness. He waits before Pilate and before Herod, and before the
Sanhedrin. He waits for the scourging and the crowning, he
waits to empty the cup of pain and dereliction. He waits for
Easter Day.

When I do meditate on the Stations it's not just some pious
remembering of Christ's passion; it's about seeing myself and
others looking back at me from these icons. This is the journey of
every person. No one is exempt.

Like Christ we will be condemned sometimes for who we are
and what we stand for and what we say and do. We will carry
the heavy burden of what it means to be human and help others
do the same. We will fall and stumble.

There will be some who care and some who don't. We will all
come to that place of stripping the spirit bare and seeing ourselves in the stark reality of our humanness, and with that sometimes awful realisation that we are disintegrating physically and
mentally. Sitting in a circle in a nursing home, fixed like Christ
to the cross, not able to walk around or feed or toilet ourselves,
staring at a notice board which tells us what day it is, and what
the weather's like and what we are going to have for dinner –
lonely, lonely road, with fewer and fewer people who come to
see us.

We will all come to this place one way or another when we
are no longer free or able to go and choose our paths – then
what? What after the shadows and the silences and the indignity
of death? The insolence of my will might lead me to doubtful
conclusions, but my rock hard faith says something different,
this cross, my cross, the world's cross …

… with its roots
in the mind's dark
was divinely planted …
(R. S. Thomas, *Amen*)

And so this book comes to its conclusion with a statement of
hope and against all the odds of my rebellious, fallen human

nature. Nothing I have in my life is really mine, everything is on loan, every person I've loved, my priesthood, my every breath. What I really desire most is to live out my God-given ministry as rent free as possible to those who might want or need what I can offer. Everything has been gift and all is harvest.

The most precious gift I have is the deep down love-faith relationship with my still elusive God. I've got used to him being that way. A lot of the more painful depth experiences have been the result of my pride-filled self-will run riot. I've looked in the past for pleasure, and now I look for joy which of its nature can contain pain and sorrow and loss and is not diminished by these things.

Making a decision to try on a daily basis to align my will to that of God has been a process of handing over everything about me that is me, to the emptiness of unknowing. I'm not fully sure who I am, but because of that I feel more confident about taking risks in my life and of being more open and generous in love. It's a wounded place to be in and always will be. There will always be the illusions and anxieties, often brought on by my own abysmal insecurity, along with my imperfect prayer life that I've tried to express in this book. I feel more inclined to bless and inspire, rather than to be filled with self-pity and anger. I wonder if ever the day will come when I don't have to explain myself to myself. I've never wanted to be pious. What I saw of piety from an early age never attracted me. Pilgrimages to sacred places have never been high on my agenda – although Lourdes because of being asked to lead a pilgrimage or two is the only place I've made a pilgrimage to. I have no desire at all to visit the Holy Land and the other places hold little for me, though I do not disparage them.

My pilgrimage has been to the centre of myself where I eventually met my God who became man in Christ in the nondescript stable, and who was discovered in the nondescript me. I like the idea of being nondescript. Some of my past Father Provincials have found me something of a conundrum, as I have too. But I cannot be anyone other than who I am, and these days I don't want to be.

I end this book, which I hope will offer something of the real possibility for everyone to be met and loved into a deeper life by this fast God of ours, with a quotation from James Alison's book *Faith beyond Resentment: Fragments Catholic and Gay*. I quote this particular piece because it says so much better than I can what all the above has been about.

These pages are written out of brokenness. This is something for which neither my theological training nor my pretensions of literacy could have prepared me. If I had escaped being broken I would indeed have written my symphonically elegant work on the 'unbinding of the gay conscience ...' And it would have been false. There is nothing elegant about inhabiting a space which has historically, socially and theologically been regarded at best risible and at worst as evil ... To speak prettily from a space that is littered with murder, with suicide and with lies is perhaps singly presumptuous ... the gift of Catholic faith kept me from killing myself ... little by little it has given me tools, the structure and the words with which to sink into, to inhabit and to begin to detoxify, at least for myself, and I hope for others, the annihilation of being.

To this hidden, quick, elusive, Bleak North of a God of mine, be all honour and praise and thanksgiving throughout all that exists for everlasting ages.

Epilogue

'The Lord blessed the latter part of Job's life more than the first.'
(Job 42:12)

And so the journey up to this point is concluded. Although for me looking over my life, there are many beginnings and many endings with no final conclusion until the last dance. I still find myself reflecting on those unfaithful moments of my life. But I trust in the one who really knows me and knows what I really want to be. I still find my God more often than not in dark places – my own and other people's.

Prayer is at the centre of things, especially the prayer of the eucharist, with its thanksgiving and its theme of sacrifice and of a body broken. All the other brokennesses of my life and of the many broken lives of others I meet, have a deep down meaning, with always the possibility of redemption, because of the eucharist, God's extravagant love made flesh. I often offer the eucharist in the darkness of early morning. I like it best like that and it's always an undeserved privilege.

I have every hope that this latter part of my life will be blessed, not with an 'easy blessing' but rather in an almost anonymous way, always aware of God's hand at work in the everyday; and always mindful of my vulnerability, always aware that I have feet of clay, and that suffering will always be part of the deal.

I hope this book on one man's experience of life, in the context of a priesthood, will offer to you the incredible possibilities of God's grace as long as there is that courage to journey to the centre of ourselves where the real 'us' is and, of course, where the kingdom of God is. All things are new every day and grace is everywhere and even if we don't have the courage for this journey, the one who loves us will make it possible somehow.

The New Year brings the old resolve
to be brave, to be patient,
to suffer the betrayal of birth
without flinching, without bitter
words. The way in was hard;
the way out could be made
easy, but one must not take
it; must await decay perhaps
of the mind, certainly of the mind's
image of itself that it has
projected. The bone aches, the blood
limps like a cripple about the ruins
of one's body. Yet what are these
but the infirmities that we share
with the creatures? It is the memories
that one has, the impenitent bungler
of love, refusing for too long
to say 'yes' to that earlier gesture
of love that had brought one
forth; it is these, as they grow
clearer with the telescoping
of the years, that constitute
for the beholder the true human pain.
(R. S. Thomas, *Resolution*)